MAKING UNEMPLOYMENT

This book is about the people who are hidden behind the unemployment statistics. What does it feel like to be put on the dole queue and to become one of the long-term unemployed? How does it feel for a teenager who has never had a job and whose mates are all in the same boat? Why are so many people out of work – and what can be done about it?

Some people feel that unemployment, like the weather, is simply a fact of life. There is nothing that we can do about it. This book disagrees. It points to positive but realistic ways forward for individual people, local groups and for national policy.

Before starting his training for ministry in the Anglican church, Dr Michael Moynagh was policy adviser on unemployment to the CBI.

As part of his work, he served as secretary to the CBI's Steering Group on Unemployment, whose members included some of Britain's leading industrialists, and travelled to the United States on behalf of the group for discussions with top industrialists, trade unionists and senior figures in the Reagan and Carter administrations.

He has been out of work for a short period himself, and has been involved in trying to start a local initiative among unemployed people. He is married with two children and lives in Bristol.

This book has been produced in association with the Shaftesbury Society, which aims to promote Christian involvement in society.

Making Unemployment Work

MICHAEL MOYNAGH

A LION PAPERBACK
Tring · Belleville · Sydney

Copyright © 1985 Lion Publishing

Published by
Lion Publishing plc
Icknield Way, Tring Herts, England
ISBN 0 85648 849 6
Albatross Books Pty Ltd
PO Box 320, Sutherland, NSW 2232, Australia
ISBN 0 86760 625 8

First edition 1985

Printed and bound in Great Britain
by Cox and Wyman, Reading

FOREWORD

As the national crisis of work deepens, the price is being paid in the poverty, depression and despair of many unemployed people and their families. It is seen in the decay and sense of dereliction of whole communities. At the same time, there is a widening gap between the well-off and the 'others'. For many people, unemployment is now a very familiar and worrying word but as yet an unfamiliar direct experience. Increasing concern about it is matched by growing feelings of helplessness. There appears to be a lack of alternatives – and not much belief in the ones that exist.

There is a great need for hope, and it must be a hope that is at the same time passionate, realistic and informed.

If we are to find the necessary will for change, many more people need to understand, and feel, what unemployment means to its victims. This books starts from there, presenting the common experience of unemployed people in a direct and telling way without trivializing them.

It is equally down-to-earth when it describes the political and economic dilemmas that lie behind the problem and when it envisages some possible answers. Amidst a welter of books on the subject it is particularly readable and free of jargon and heavy statistics. The author recognizes that change is needed at many levels, in heart and will, attitude and institution, but that it *is* possible and that we have to start somewhere. There are sections both on a possible national strategy to deal with unemployment and on taking local action, and both show a hopeful realism.

This book should be very widely read, especially by those people who feel relatively untouched by unemployment. It is written out of Christian concern, and will appeal to all who are concerned to find new, real answers to this burning problem of our time. It challenges our feelings of helplessness and points to spiritual and moral themes that can orientate us in our response to unemployment. I think it will repay both individual and group study and I am very pleased to commend it.

David Sheppard,
Bishop of Liverpool

ACKNOWLEDGMENTS

Many people have made this book possible. Ogilvy & Mather conducted in-depth surveys with some fifty unemployed people in 1982. I am grateful to them and to the Confederation of British Industry, which commissioned the study, for allowing me to use the transcripts of the interviews. Many of the case studies which appear in the book are based on these interviews, though names have been changed to preserve anonymity. In one or two cases I have taken the liberty of building a story around a person, to emphasize an important point.

I began to think seriously about unemployment while working at the CBI, and gained valuable insights from the work of their Steering Group on Unemployment, to which I was secretary. I acknowledge a debt to my colleagues there, in particular to John Cahill who taught me a great deal. I have also benefitted from discussions with various groups of unemployed people.

The book was written while studying theology at Trinity College, Bristol. The college provided a convivial atmosphere in which to undertake the work. I learnt much from various members of staff, especially the Rev. Mark Geldard, whose lectures on the theology of work set me off on new trains of thought. Involvement in a college proposal for a community project with the unemployed (currently thwarted through shortage of MSC funds) raised issues connected with local action on unemployment.

The further reading section at the end of the book shows how much I owe to others who have worked in this area. I am also grateful for helpful comments from the following who read all or part of the book in draft: John Cahill, Rev. Julian Charley, Rev. Mark Geldard, Mrs Rachel Hindley, Roy McCloughry, David Mundy, Adrian Newman, Rev. Francis Palmer and Professor Adrian Sinfield.

My wife Liz did a fantastic job turning indecipherable script into legible type. She did an even better job of providing precious love and invaluable support. To her, and to Felicity and Simon, I owe the greatest debt of all – for the cost of the time taken to write the book has fallen heaviest on them.

Michael Moynagh

CONTENTS

CHAPTER 1

The Unemployment Experience

A CASE OF DESPAIR

Each weekday Malcolm leaves his comfortable lego-built house in a London suburb. His wife drives him to the station where he catches the train to work. At the other end he joins the white-collar tide rushing to the office. In the evening he hurries back to the station, carries the day's preoccupations onto the train, and is met by his wife waiting to drive him home. The only unemployed person Malcolm sees that day appears in a TV programme he happens to watch.

One of the curses of unemployment is that so few people – even with today's high numbers out of work – feel directly affected by it. Many, like Malcolm, live their ordinary lives hardly coming across the jobless, scarcely imagining the anguish of being without work. They can acknowledge the problem in their heads without actually feeling the bewilderment that accompanies the shock of being made redundant, the stabs of pain that follow the rejection of one job application after another, and the emptiness that accompanies life in a vacuum. They are nicely distanced from the problem. They need never be stirred emotionally by it.

Across the luxury gap lives George Stevens, a forty-five-year-old welder who has been out of work for eighteen months. Unemployment is no stranger to the Newcastle community where he lives. This is the third generation of people who have either known unemployment in their own family or in the family of close friends. 'Like most of the other people I have interviewed', commented a researcher into the experience of unemployment, 'Mr Stevens doesn't really feel that he himself can do a lot about the problems of unemployment, and indeed that the government and employees can do very much either. He doesn't therefore believe that he ought to be doing anything. So the failure to do anything, or to know what it is that one ought to do, is not really considered a failure in any sense.'

George illustrates a common response to unemployment – the feeling of impotence, of being overwhelmed by a massive problem. Put his type of reaction alongside the emotional indifference of people in work like Malcolm, and one can begin to understand why unemployment has been greeted in the early 1980s by a widespread mood of resignation. True, the mood has been punctuated by the odd flash of anger, such as the feeling that 'something must be done' following the Toxteth riots in 1981. And even now there is mounting opinion that policies must be changed. Yet among many people there is still a prevailing despair which says there is little option but to continue as we are.

The purpose of this book is to show that this is not the case. Much can be done to combat unemployment. There *are* strategies which would greatly reduce the size of the problem today and mould tomorrow's patterns of work and leisure in exciting ways. What these strategies require, however, is the will to act.

Commitment is particularly important from people like Malcolm. They have the money which – if they were willing – could be used to improve the lot of the unemployed. (The take-home pay of those in work rose faster between 1979 and 1984, allowing for inflation, than at any time since the war.) They have the work which – if they were ready to do so – could be shared with the unemployed. And they elect MPs who – if they were forced by public opinion – could ensure that more was done to tackle unemployment. Those in areas of relatively low unemployment have the means and collectively the power to attack the problem. But why should they bother?

In the 1960s and 1970s the answer was easy. If unemployment was to rise to the unthinkable level of 3 to 4 million, it was said, people would riot in the streets and society would tear at the seams. Self-interest demanded action to keep the number of jobless down. Today the situation is different. The unthinkable has happened. And those outside the areas gnawed by unemployment see few signs of social decay. Their lives have been scarcely affected. One person in a position of influence remarked how strange it was that he could not see the unemployed today. The comment was unsurprising from someone who lived in Chelsea and was chauffeur-driven to work in central London!

So often those with secure jobs living in affluent suburbs are heard to say, 'Anyone can find work if they look for it.' They dismiss unemployment as a self-inflicted condition rather than a state imposed on the unwilling victim by economic forces beyond his or her control. It is precisely the invisibility of the jobless to such people that is the difficulty. If you feel untouched by a problem you are not likely to try to understand it – let alone bear the costs of any solution.

That is why it is important for those who have jobs to get under the skin of the unemployed, to imagine the experience of being without work for themselves. Then they will be able to feel – if only to a small extent – something of the misery involved. Of course they can, if they want, ignore the problem altogether, which would be callous. Or they can imaginatively feel the problem and then ignore it, which would be brutal. Or they can make the problem their own, identify with the unemployed and make sacrifices to alleviate the suffering involved – the suffering of people like Jim.

STEPS INTO DESPAIR

Jim had worked as a plastic extruder for eighteen years. His company made transfusion units and other medical equipment for hospitals. Up to 1980, business was so brisk with night shifts and weekend work, that, as Jim said, 'you could literally live there if you wanted to.'

Then came the government health cuts. Restrictions were placed on the amount the health service could spend on new equipment. Business plummeted and Jim's section was completely closed down. Jim was stunned. 'You feel as though someone's kicked you in the stomach,' he said later. The blow was so great that he just could not take it in. He kept saying to himself, 'This can't be true. It's not me they're getting rid of after all these years. And not my mates as well.' For a day or two he felt quite numbed by it all. He simply could not focus his mind on what had happened. He was confused, and occasionally felt cold all over.

Shock

Jim's shock was hardly surprising. Redundancy meant more than the loss of a job – it threatened his whole way of life. And with other local companies closing down or laying people off, the threat was very real. At fifty-three, Jim was unlikely to get another job. He was faced with a whole series of losses: the daily company of his workmates, an income, a reason for getting up in the morning, his status as breadwinner in the eyes of family and friends, and his sense of competence in doing a job well. It was only natural that his first instinct should be to try to distance himself from the event so that he would not have to experience its full impact. He could not have coped with the emotional trauma of being brought face to face with the full reality of being out of work. The pain would have been literally too great to bear, hence the feeling of numbness as Jim's mind tried to protect his emotions.

Shock is a common response to the loss of a job, especially when the loss is sudden and the attachment to the job is particularly great (in this case because the person has held it for many years). Jim needed plenty of support during those first few days. He needed to be allowed to let the reality of what had happened sink in slowly, so that he could begin to come to terms with it in his own time. He would then be ready to take the first tentative steps towards facing the situation.

Denial

For the next few weeks Jim's family were taken aback by his optimism. Once the shock had passed, Jim seemed so euphoric. 'At least I know the worst. Now I can talk about it,' he said. 'It's great. At last I'm free to do what I want. Look at all these jobs round the house I haven't had time to do. It's fantastic! Now I can do them.' He suggested spending his redundancy money on a family holiday in Majorca. When Jim's wife Brenda talked about finding a job, Jim said he would have no difficulty 'when the time comes'. He thought to himself, 'A lot of people who are unemployed are only willing to do jobs they are used to. They're quite different from me. I'm flexible. When things get a bit tough, I can turn my hand to anything.'

This optimism (events would show how false it was) represented Jim's first stumbling attempt to come to terms with what had happened. During the shock phase, the unemployed person may be too numb even to begin to understand what has occurred, but in the denial phase he or she starts to search for an explanation. However, the person's emotions may not be ready to take in the possibility of how much has been lost. They need to hang on to the pretence that very little has changed in practice.

The idea, shared by many at the beginning of their unemployment, that being out of work is like a holiday, fits this need particularly well. The transition between jobs (they assume that they *will* find another job) can be presented to themselves and to their family and friends as being the same as a holiday. Nothing has really changed. 'I'll soon find a job,' the person imagines, 'just like the one before – with the same sort of pay, using the same skills. And if the worst comes to the worst, there is plenty of other work around.'

This denial of reality is a form of psychological armour which protects the individual from the deep wound he or she would experience if confronted too early by the full truth of the situation. It provides a cover story to shield their emotions. This helps to explain the tendency for redundancy pay often to be splashed on lavish holidays and other luxuries. People who have not experienced unemployment are frequently surprised by this. But if people feel the need to pretend that nothing has changed, then they must act as if nothing has changed. They feel on holiday, so they must go on holiday. If they have received a cash windfall, then they must spend it in the way they would if they were still at work. It is not unknown for the unemployed to leave home each morning as if going to work and to return at the normal time in the evening, without telling their wives they have lost their job. They feel a need to keep up the pretence that nothing has changed.

The only thing that temporarily shattered Jim's make-believe was signing on for the dole. The first time he went, Jim had to sign on at the Unemployment Benefit Office to secure his entitlement to unemployment benefit. Because he had a wife and child who were financially dependent on him, he also went to the separate Supplementary Benefits Office, where he was means-tested to see if he was entitled to an additional supplementary benefit payment (plus rent and other allowances). His third port of call was the Job Centre, where registration was obligatory for those drawing unemployment benefit up to 1982, but is now voluntary. The whole experience was frustrating because there was so much waiting involved (it took a complete morning), and was deeply humiliating.

'I'd never actually done it before,' Jim said later. 'I found it very degrading actually...I went in the inquiries-type place and they told me to take a seat, and I saw these cubicle-type things – it's not even private, you know. Anyway, you sit down and she calls. You go to one of these cubicles (it reminded me of a horse box), and then you've got to fill out all these forms and then you have to go somewhere else... The worst thing about it is that there is nothing private about it. You've no interest while you hang about down there and wait, and there are queues of people. It's a horrible experience... You're just a number.'

To be means-tested for supplementary benefit can be an extremely painful experience, especially for older workers who had steady jobs and expect to be able to look after their families. Unlike supplementary benefit, unemployment benefit is given as a right for up to one year if the person has paid enough contributions while at work. However, the level of benefit is frequently not enough to meet the subsistence needs of unemployed families. In such cases supplementary benefit and a housing allowance may be paid as well. Supplementary benefit is also available to those who have not paid enough contributions, or to those who have been out of work for more than a year and have stopped getting unemployment benefit. In practice, some three-quarters of the jobless claiming benefit of some kind receive supplementary benefit.

All this makes for a very confusing system, which is bad enough for someone out of work. But far worse is the fact that supplementary benefit is paid only if the person's other sources of income are less than their subsistence needs – in other words, if they cannot keep themselves or their family. Filling in forms to demonstrate that you are poor can be a crippling blow to your self-esteem. The unemployed have to prove that they cannot cope – that they are failures (in terms of today's values) at a time when they are trying to flee any suggestion that this might be the case. The person who feels inadequate because he has lost his job finds his nose rubbed in his sense of worthlessness.

This is particularly true in areas where comparatively few are out of work or where high unemployment is a recent experience. Because such communities expect people to have jobs, admitting that you cannot look after your family can be extremely painful. In places of persistent high unemployment, on the other hand, the unemployed can take comfort from knowing that many of their friends are in the same boat.

To get benefit the unemployed have to sign on within a week of losing their job. But this is precisely the time when many are not yet ready to face reality fully. This was certainly the case with Jim. To him, the perspex window between the dole queue and the official behind represented the difference between those who were in their jobs and those who were out. Facing the perspex window brought him face to face with his own unemployment. He could pretend he was on holiday till he joined the dole queue. Then the awful reality struck him. The length of the queue might comfort some: there are others in the same position. But for Jim it was a reminder that he was no longer an employee, just a number. It underlined how difficult it might be to get work: 'they're all in competition with me'. For a short while his cover story was blown.

Being forced to face reality before he was ready to do so was a very cruel experience for Jim. It was one reason why, like many others out of work, he felt so much resentment at signing on. Sometimes people are surprised that those behind the perspex windows often face bitter abuse from the unemployed. But it is an abuse born partly from making people face a reality that they cannot face.

Search

After about three weeks Jim felt he had to start looking for work. After all, he thought, a holiday cannot go on for ever. His cover story depended on a belief that he was in a holiday-like transition between jobs. At some stage Jim had to put that belief to the test. His unemployment experience had to enter its next phase – the search for a job.

Some see 'denial' and 'search' as a single optimistic phase, while others describe 'search' as part of the next phase of 'despair'. But 'search' can also be viewed as a distinct phase between the two. It is a step beyond optimism as the individual tests out his or her interpretation of what has happened. Is he right to think that he is in a short transition between jobs? Is it true that she will not have too much difficulty in finding work once she starts to look? Now is the time to find out. Equally (at least to begin with) it is not a time of despair. The person is still sure that he or she will get a job. It is only when repeated job knock-backs leave them psychologically knocked-out that it becomes clear how far their optimism has shielded them from the true despair of their situation.

This was the first time Jim fully confronted the reality of his situation. He hoped initially to get a plastic extruding job similar to the one he had lost. But a few days scanning the ads convinced him that this was not on. He had to lower his sights. He started to look for jobs that paid less than his previous one and required different (often fewer) skills.

Contrary to a quite common belief that some people remain out of work because they have unreasonably high job expectations, Jim's response was typical of most of the unemployed. Research shows that those without jobs are generally quite flexible in the type of work they seek. They are willing to apply for jobs at a lower level and using different skills to the ones they have left. They are prepared to take a drop in earnings. But there is a minimum income below which they will not go. For men, according to a survey in 1980, this seemed to be between £65 and £74 a week after tax, which was considerably more than most took home in benefits.

Over the next five weeks Jim applied for fifteen jobs. He was short-listed for two. For one he had the wrong qualifications. At the other they had 'all my qualifications and references. And then they said, "date of birth?" And then it's "Oh, I'm sorry, we don't employ anybody over fifty. You're too old." It makes me feel pig-sick, sick as a pig.' Jim's family watched a new mood come over him. His former confidence gave way to a sober realism, which gradually turned into sullen despair. He became angry towards those who rejected his applications, and increasingly pessimistic about getting a job.

Later, Jim would see this period as a time of wasted opportunity. Each day he used to wait eagerly for the post. Would this be the day when he heard that he had been short-listed, perhaps even got a job? Many employers, however, did not even tell him that he had been turned down. With so many applicants for each job, employers claim they cannot afford to write to everyone they reject. So people like Jim are kept waiting, almost indefinitely, hoping against hope that tomorrow will be the day... One person hated not hearing so much that with each job application he enclosed a stamped addressed envelope and a typed rejection note for the manager to sign. In most cases not even these were returned. But on one of the exceptions he found scrawled: 'I couldn't have written a better rejection note myself. You'll go far.'

Jim's hope that he would get a job prevented him facing the possibility that he could be out of work for a long time. As a result, he missed an opportunity to find alternative ways of coping with unemployment. As he later admitted, while morale was high he could have gone round the local day centres to see what voluntary work was available. He might have been more keen to discover what casual jobs were around. He might have looked more carefully at those part-time jobs he ignored in the expectation of finding a full-time one. None of these would have compensated for the lack of well-paid work. But they would have been better than the horizon of emptiness that Jim faced when it gradually dawned on him how difficult getting a job would be. As he began to despair, he became more lethargic. He lost the energy to look for second-best solutions.

Despair

'What is the worst part of knowing you won't get a job?' Jim found it difficult to answer. There were so many ugly features it was hard to know which was worst. There was, for a start, the feeling of utter failure. 'You just feel inadequate,' Jim sighed. 'All I get is this cheque and the only job I've got is to sign the cheque once a fortnight to get the dough. It's nothing. You just feel totally wasted...useless.' One job rejection after another inevitably makes one feel a reject. Jim's inability to support his family was an acute blow to his pride. On top of that, Brenda, his wife, had recently found a job. Jim felt it was degrading. 'The tables have been turned, and it's not really what you got married for, is it? We're supposed to keep them!'

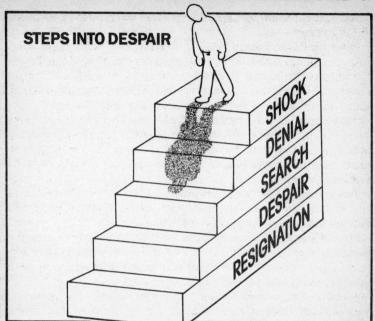

STEPS INTO DESPAIR

SHOCK
DENIAL
SEARCH
DESPAIR
RESIGNATION

This sense of personal failure is made worse by the isolation that unemployment brings. 'When I went out for a drink, my mates knew that I was out of work, so they'd say, "Go on, Jim. I'll buy you a drink," on the quiet, like. And it was awful – even on a Saturday night. You knew it couldn't go on like that. It's stopped me going out now... When I was at work I had quite a few friends actually, but they were friends at work. I got all the male side of friendship from my work, you know, so that when I came home again it was a nice change to speak to the wife, kind of thing. But now I'm basically more in a woman's world, being at home.' Even that had changed since Brenda got a job. Jim's isolation was greater than ever. Loneliness often drives the jobless on to the streets in a desperate attempt to be with people. Some feel compelled to go shopping each day – an expensive hobby if you are living on benefit.

This isolation stems largely from the financial hardship experienced by the unemployed. Like Jim, they cannot afford to join their mates for a drink or take part in other social activities. The worry and frustration of being hard-up comes across time after time in conversations with the jobless. Jim was hardly well-off at work. He reckoned he would be ticking over though, putting aside a bit for this, a quid for that, with no real worries about the rates, electricity and so on. 'But on the dole,' he said, 'you're not ticking over at all. You're scratching.' The scratching is worse for those with a mortgage, hire-purchase agreements, or other long-standing commitments to meet.

Few unemployed people can draw on private financial reserves. Contrary to a widely-held view, lump sum payments (including redundancy pay) made to the unemployed on leaving their jobs are generally small, if they are paid at all. Over a quarter of those who left their jobs in mid-1980 received no extra payment; about a quarter got less than £100; and a further quarter received between £100 and £500.

Few of the unemployed have many savings – and if these exceed £3,000 their supplementary benefit is cut. Many people who lose jobs as they approach retirement experience sheer horror when they find that they get nothing at all after their first year if they have saved £3,000 or more (and this even includes the surrender value of life insurance policies). Knowledge that their hard-earned savings count against them fills them with deep resentment. It seems that thrift is being penalized.

Often those without jobs can expect little financial support from other members of the family. The proportion of wives of the unemployed who are working is about half that of the population as a whole. In high unemployment spots it is common to find dole-full families – homes where everyone is out of work. Frequently, in places where parents are more likely to have jobs, the young unemployed living at home are still expected to contribute to the family purse.

Apart from a few casual and undeclared earnings on the side, the jobless depend heavily on state benefits. An unemployed family with two children receives an income of about two-fifths of average earnings. Someone who is single is likely to get about a quarter of what the average person with a job has left after paying tax and travelling expenses. Some three-fifths of the jobless are single. In 1980, Reg Prentice, Minister of State at the Department of Health and Social Security, said about supplementary benefit for the unemployed: 'What is provided now and has always been provided is inadequate. I accept that.' Yet at that very moment the government was making the situation worse by phasing out the unemployment benefit's earnings-related supplement, which had boosted the incomes of many out of work considerably. At the time of writing, it is reported that the British government wants to hack back even further the real value of benefits received by the jobless.

Then there is the sheer boredom of being without a job. Lack of money makes it difficult enough for the unemployed to find something to do. One church set up an unemployed art class which uncovered all sorts of talent among redundant men who had not done anything like it before. The organizer remarked casually as she showed a friend around, 'Of course, they cannot move into oils because they cannot afford it.' And as if shortage of cash was not enough, the inability to get a job frequently destroys both the self-confidence and the incentive to seek imaginative pastimes which can be afforded.

Jim found that DIY, which had been fun when it was a break from work, seemed rather pointless once it had become his main activity. Little interests had been fine when they had been the icing on the cake. But when they became the cake itself, they were far too sweet. 'If this is all there is to life,' he thought, 'how useless my life has become.'

Jim's concept of time changed dramatically. Days seemed to fly past with nothing to distinguish them or remember them by. Visits to the Job Centre became less frequent. 'It's like a continuous weekend,' he said. Often he would lose track of the time. He slept much more than he used to – up to fourteen hours a day sometimes. This irritated the family who felt he should be getting up earlier. 'I wish you would make more of an effort,' Brenda would say. 'No one will give you a job if you're lying in bed.'

But for Jim, sleep was the only way to cut out the darkness of the day. Being awake, he said, 'could be hell'. The sight of others in the street setting off for work in the morning reminded him that this is what he ought to be doing. He felt such a failure. That thought had become the recurring theme of his life. There were no other interests to crowd it out. Better to sleep, Jim thought. At least with sleep came oblivion.

Resignation

'I think,' Jim said later, 'you reach the stage where – it's difficult to explain – but you get to the state when you worry yourself stupid. You think it's got to be next week, or the week after when you'll get a job. But then as time goes on, you get past the worrying stage. You see there is no point in worrying about it. Your whole life becomes this signing on – that is the real life now. So you get into this routine where you just live from day to day. You look forward to stupid little things which give you pleasure, and you carry on. You get a sort of patience about the whole thing.'

This is the phase of resignation. The person passively accepts his or her fate. The anxiety and depression of the 'despair' phase lifts, and the individual settles down to new standards and a different way of life. Feelings of inferiority and submissiveness become more marked. The person seems less able to provide for his or her needs. The search for a job becomes still more haphazard, and may cease altogether. 'I suppose it's a fault,' Jim remarked. 'I used really to fight for things, but I don't any more. I just don't really feel interested in fighting for things any more.' This has been aptly described as 'the broken state'.

Over 1.2 million people in Britain have been out of work for a year or more. Many will have reached this broken state. If they happen to get a job interview – perhaps through a friend – they will be so sure of failure that they will present an attitude of not caring anyway. If it does not matter, then the rejection will feel less painful. The interviewer's natural response will be 'Well, if you don't care, why should I?' and he will hire someone else instead. The failure will become a self-fulfilling prophecy. The demoralization of many long-term unemployed makes it specially hard for them to respond to measures designed to help them. They frequently lack the motivation to join or stay on programmes. Their lethargy and apparent ill-discipline may have to be countered with infinite patience, close supervision and strong incentives.

It is during this final phase that the accumulated effects on health of being without work may become most apparent. A survey of nearly 1,000 jobless people showed a tendency to take longer over things, to concentrate less on what they were doing, to become rusty at things they once did well, to have greater difficulty in remembering things and to find it harder to make decisions. Poignantly, one in five said they had lost the ability to crack a joke. One in ten experienced a deterioration in physical health, including worsening angina, back problems, bronchitis, headaches, high blood pressure and ulcers.

People have sometimes been surprised that the unemployed have not rioted more in the streets. There are of course those, mainly the young, who resort to crime as a way to bring excitement and meaning back to a life devoid of interest. On many housing estates, crime has jumped by an alarming amount, the rise in violent crime being especially frightening. But this is not a typical response to unemployment. The bulk of the jobless have accepted their lot more passively. The reason is not hard to understand. Those who are shocked or who try to put a brave face on reality are not likely to rebel against it. And those who are crushed by despair or resigned to the inevitable are hardly the stuff of which revolutions are made.

DIFFERENT DOSES OF DESPAIR

Jim's story is really a model of how many writers have seen the experience of being out of work. Drawing mainly on studies of unemployment in the 1930s, they have portrayed the experience in terms of stages. The number of stages, which are acknowledged to be somewhat arbitrary, varies between three and seven, according to the writer's taste.

It is helpful to describe unemployment in these terms. A great many people without jobs will go through several (though not perhaps all) the stages of shock, denial, search, despair and resignation described here. Realizing that their feelings are normal can be a great encouragement to them. And recognition of what is going on (which is rather like the experience of bereavement after losing a loved one) can help family and friends to provide appropriate support. Perhaps it is worth emphasizing, too, that although we have taken Jim as our example, for many women unemployment can be just as painful an experience.

More recently, writers have tended to place greater stress on the variations in how people react to being out of work. No one experience will be exactly the same as another. Often it will be very different. A seventeen-year-old completing a youth training scheme with little expectation of getting a job may suffer virtually no shock on joining the dole queue. For her father, however, redundancy may come as a devastating blow. The degree and nature of the despair may vary, too. The seventeen-year-old's despair may focus on her lost hopes for the future. Aware of the competition for jobs, she may have struggled especially hard to get those 'O' levels which would put her ahead in the job marathon. Her sense that the struggle has been in vain may be every bit as painful as her father's rather different feeling of rejection on being made redundant after twenty years' service. So what will determine how a person responds to unemployment?

Obviously, **the nature of the individual's personality** is important. Jim showed a fair degree of persistence in pursuing the job hunt for even three weeks. Many have so little self-confidence that, even in areas where quite a few jobs are around, they despair of getting one almost before they have begun to look. Where unemployment is relatively low, many of the jobless have a history of failure behind them. Often they have been in the lowest streams at school, got few if any qualifications, have been forced into the lowest paid jobs (if they found work at all) and have discovered that for one reason or another these jobs were only temporary anyway. Used to failure, they expect it to continue. Their motivation is low because their self-confidence is low. It is not surprising that some skip the search stage almost completely and drift rapidly into the stage of despair.

Others may find that unemployment comes when they are feeling particularly vulnerable. Their **stage in the life-cycle** may reduce their ability to cope. Parents with children ready to leave home will be facing the prospect of not being needed in the same way as before. The children are likely to be challenging family norms – the son, perhaps, not getting out of Dad's usual chair when he comes into the room. For the father, redundancy at this stage may pose a particular threat to his self-esteem. Already vulnerable, he may now feel even less able to cope with the changes ahead. He may find himself lashing out more often in anger at his son's 'impudence'.

For a son or daughter, failure to get a job may be traumatic in an entirely different way. Starting work may be one of the traditional signs in their community that they have become adults. A job would normally provide, too, the income they need to become more independent of home. Unemployment may force them into a continuing family dependence at a time when they should be breaking free.

The manner of joining the dole queue can affect people's responses to unemployment. In Jim's case, his whole section was made redundant. He found this bad enough, but it would be even worse if he had been the only one in his section to go. He would be left with the nagging suspicion that he had been sacked because he was not up to the job. Self-doubt about his own competence might fuel his sense of personal failure at not finding work.

Added to this, if Jim thought he had been forced to leave unfairly, resentment would probably fester. 'I'd have been all right if it hadn't been for the supervisor', he might think. With no other way to express it, this resentment might turn towards the family: 'They're against me, too.' Outbursts of anger against relatives would understandably encourage them to keep their distance, increasing Jim's isolation and his bitterness. But how different it would be if Jim could have taken voluntary redundancy. Then, his self-esteem might have taken less of a knock. At least he could claim that he had never suffered the indignity of being forced to leave.

The nature of a particular job will also influence how the person responds to its loss. People in the building trade who are used to being laid off between jobs are unlikely to find the break a particular shock. They may see it as part of the established routine of the trade. They could well miss out the phases of shock and optimism and start immediately to look for alternative work. Only as the search proves fruitless may it dawn on them, as they slide into despair, that this time it is different. Quite a few people may be in this position. In terms of previous job, those who worked in construction comprise the largest single group among the unemployed.

What happened to Phil illustrates a different influence on the recently-unemployed. Phil had achieved a position of status among his friends at work on Tyneside and in his family by becoming a blacksmith. This had involved a five-year apprenticeship which equipped him with a high level of skill in his craft and the ability to undertake work requiring a lot of physical and mental strength. Phil communicated this by his sturdy build and the confidence with which he related to people. Because Phil's self-esteem was so bound up with the job, redundancy shattered his confidence. Far more than loss of a job was involved: Phil's whole view of himself as a strong, masculine person was at stake.

Phil might have felt less threatened had he possessed **the ability to identify with other socially acceptable roles**. If he had been coming up to retirement age, for example, he could have presented himself to family and friends as having retired early. Involving little loss of dignity, this new status would have helped to protect his self-esteem. At nearly half the age of retirement, however, that option was not open to him. Becky, by contrast, is married with two teenage children. She went back to work several years ago, but the factory was recently closed. She now describes herself as a housewife, which is far from ideal, but better than saying she is unemployed.

Many people, of course, cannot redefine their roles in this way. They are forced to describe themselves as unemployed. How far this label is felt to be personally humiliating can be influenced by **the level of unemployment in the locality**. The fewer out of work, the greater is likely to be the personal stigma attached to unemployment. Greater will be the felt disgrace of having to sign on every fortnight, of admitting to friends that you are out work and of telling the family that you 'failed' yet another job interview.

In areas of high unemployment, however, signing on will be a normal part of the community's life. All sorts of survival strategies will have been pioneered. Knowledge of how to play the social security system will be widespread. Younger people especially may draw comfort from the fact that many of their school friends are also out of work. Yet the pain of unemployment does not disappear. It may be felt less acutely as a personal stigma, but it receives a stronger community expression instead. The neighbourhood becomes drab and despondent, the streets appear to be run down as housing decays – there's no money to keep it smart. Anyone going anywhere clears out. The individual's despair turns into a community malaise.

Again, responses to the situation will not be the same. Much will depend on a final, crucial factor: **the strength of family and community ties**. In parts of Birmingham, where recent high-rise blocks have destroyed entire communities, unemployment can be a bitterly lonely experience. An unemployed man, whose wife does not work, may feel that he is on his own in the world. He may have the support of good friends, but he alone is responsible for his family. His wife is isolated, too. Even if they are a local family, redevelopment makes it unlikely that they live near their parents, or next door to uncles, cousins, sisters and brothers. When anger explodes in these circumstances, it smashes the windows of strangers.

In a place like Hartlepool though, where the absence of busy planners has left the streets virtually untouched, the extended family still flourishes and is acquiring a new role. Usually it has at least one member still in paid work. Operating as a single unit, the benefits of this are shared around to provide a cushion for members without jobs. Cars are loaned, small sums exchange hands, an employed son may ensure that his father has the price of a pint at the end of the week. Opportunities for casual work (which will not be declared to the DHSS lest benefits are cut) are shared around the family. If a young mother gets some work in the launderette, other members will mind the children.

No longer is the extended family run by women mainly to meet male needs. Increasingly, unemployed men, as well as women, will help those of whatever sex who have work. But there are, it seems, limits. The father may look after the toddler, but refuse to take care of the child in nappies. He may help to wash the dishes, but not the clothes. Yet even so, the home has become less of a bolt-hole for the man exhausted by grinding work, and more a place where the unwaged are recognized as contributing members of the family rather than as numbers on the register. Just as the benefits of unemployment are distributed around the family, so the misery of unemployment is shared instead of being concentrated on the individual.

Sometime people ask, 'Why don't the unemployed move to where the jobs are? Why stay in an area of hardly any work when jobs can be found further afield?' The answer is simple. People's roots are often deep in a locality. The extended family can provide a comradeship to replace that of work, a network of financial support and the possibility of access to paid work in the future. There is little point in moving to an area you do not know, where there are no family and friends to provide support and where housing may be considerably more expensive. To get 'on yer bike' and leave home would be madness.

BRINGING DESPAIR HOME

This example from Hartlepool illustrates not only how the family can help the individual to adjust to unemployment, but also how the individual's unemployment affects the family. But these are short-term changes. If high levels of unemployment continue over a long period, what long-term changes in family patterns might we expect? At present, we do not know enough about the effects of unemployment on family life to be sure, but the changes may be quite profound. Family roles may alter permanently, with fathers being more involved in 'domestic' chores. Couples increasingly may wait longer before having children because of delays in finding stable employment and establishing the home. Unemployment can, for example, postpone a couple's move away from parents to a place of their own.

Far more clear, however, is the immediate impact of unemployment on the family. This is how one fifty-three-year-old described it: 'All of a sudden you become unemployed, and you're upsetting their system 'cause you're not supposed to be sitting there in the morning. So it's "shift your feet, I want to get the hoover underneath", which is understandable. But you're fed up, and they are because you are upsetting their system and the thing they've always been doing for years. You're still always there when they come back. It makes you feel in the bloody way.' The family's irritation threshold falls. Petty differences erupt into full-scale rows as frustration mounts. This is particularly so where the couple used to live quite independent lives – with husband, say, down at the pub most evenings. Husband and wife may get on each other's nerves now that they spend more time together. How they resolve the situation will reflect largely the strengths and weaknesses of their relationship.

In other families, the husband may try to shield his family from the full impact of what has happened. He may try to hide the seriousness of it. One disabled forty-four-year-old, who had been out or work for two years, could not bear to tell his children about his unemployment. 'They harass me – they ask what type of work I'm doing. I tell them I'm still doing security work, but they keep asking, "When do you pay for our dinners then?" because they have free school meals 'cause of my supplmentary benefit. When I see other children – their parents are working, they've got a car and everything like that – that's when I, I don't sleep...' As in this case, attempts to disguise the truth normally fail. They serve merely to prevent the family facing the problem as a unit. The man is deprived of support from within the family, increasing his isolation.

The effects of long-term unemployment on children are almost incalculable. The children may resent having to go to work at school while Daddy is seen to do nothing all day. In areas where unemployment is not so common, their father's loss of personal worth is likely to rub off on the children. They feel a loss of prestige and try to disguise their father's unemployment from their friends. Their drop in self-confidence may then in turn be reflected by anti-social behaviour or lack of progress at school. In areas of high unemployment, lack of hope can lower the expectations of even young children. One teacher in the West Midlands has six and seven-year-olds saying to her, 'What is the use of working, Miss, when I'll never get a job?'

Then there are the effects of prolonged unemployment on the children's physical health. For those with younger children, malnutrition can have devastating effects. A study of 10,000 children found that two-year-old toddlers of the long-term unemployed were up to an inch shorter than other children. Significantly more child abuse was reported in Corby following the closure of the town's steel works in 1981.

CONCLUSION

Unemployment is about despair, poverty, feelings of failure, frustration and sometimes violence within the family. Who can tell what the full affects will be on the children worst affected? Unless those in jobs can catch some of the despair and feel the misery involved, unemployment will never be tackled effectively. Successful strategies will require the commitment of those in work, for as we shall see the most promising solution will demand the sharing of wealth and jobs. But why should the more fortunate share their good fortune? The answer lies in the number of desperate people, crushed under the weight of unemployment, who need jobs not just to live the good life – but to have a quality of life at all.

While work spells self-esteem, money, confidence and friendships, unemployment often equals shock, false optimism, search, despair and resignation. The response may vary according to personality, stage of life, how one joined the dole queue, the nature of the previous job, whether he or she can assume other socially acceptable roles, the level of unemployment in the area and the support available from family and friends. But whatever its form, despair is almost invariably present and is likely to affect others in the family. To be moved by a vision of how work can be created, we need first to capture a vision of how lives can be emptied by the absence of work.

CHAPTER 2

Who is Out of Work?

Mark Rankin of the Volunteer Centre spends a lot of time with self-help groups among the jobless. These are groups of unemployed people who come together for mutual support and encouragement. 'Recently, I was with a fairly typical group of prematurely retired businessmen, blacks, feminists, redundant factory workers and several very depressed people. For an afternoon the group struggled to decide on a common strategy. Unsurprisingly, we failed to agree.' It seems that the group was something of a shambles. There were too many people with very different needs and backgrounds to allow it to unite around a common task.

It is vital to remember that the jobless cannot be lumped together under the label 'unemployed' and treated as a single group. There will be a world of difference between the needs and experiences of the skilled and unskilled, of the teenager and his fifty-five-year-old father, of those who have been out of work for two weeks and people unemployed for two years, between men and women, and so on. Whether action is being planned at a local level by some voluntary group or at a national level by government, they must decide which group of the unemployed they are aiming for. The programme must then be tailored to the needs of the target group. If the aim is to help older job-seekers, then the programme should obviously avoid heavy physical work more suited to the young!

But designing projects for particular groups raises the awkward question of priorities. Why plan a scheme for the old rather than the under twenty-fives? Should the young who are normally single have priority over the middle-aged with families to support? Should we concentrate on preventing the recently unemployed staying out of work for a long time, or direct our efforts toward the long-term unemployed? How much attention should be given to the needs of ethnic minorities? Dilemmas like these arise because governments and voluntary groups never have enough money to do all that they want to do. They have to choose between different groups among the jobless.

THE UNEMPLOYMENT POOL

Some people think unemployment is like a scrap heap. A person is no longer required at work, becomes disposable and is dumped on the heap where he or she stays for evermore. School-leavers or those completing youth training schemes get left on the pile, too, because no jobs are available for them. Phrases like 'a generation who have never worked' betray this view. However, this picture is grossly distorted. Only a minority drop onto the heap never to work again, though the numbers in this category are growing. Some two-thirds of the unemployed will get jobs within a year of 'signing on'. There is a constant movement in and out of unemployment.

This movement could be seen as a pool. The unemployed enter the pool, swim around in it for a while and then flow out again when they find a job. Such a picture would have been a very apt description of British unemployment in the late 1960s, for example, when the number out of work for a year or more was around 70,000, more than one in seven of those queuing for the dole. The situation today is very different. In 1984, 1.2 million people had been without a job for at least a year, roughly the number of people living in Birmingham. They represented one in every three people looking for work. In other words, although today's unemployment is like a pool in that many people are flowing in and out, there are others who never escape, or who stay in it for a very long time.

A more accurate picture of unemployment would be a pool with a thick layer of sand at the bottom. The bulk of the unemployed flow into the pool and out again within a year. About a third, however, sink to the bottom. They are described as the long-term unemployed – people who have been without jobs for at least a year. Their experience is rather like that of falling to the bottom of a pool. There they lie, immersed in unemployment. But just as beautiful plants grow from sand in a pool, so from today's unemployment can spring hope for the future – provided we take the opportunities. That is the theme of this book.

THE SAND
The unskilled

If we lower a camera into the pool to get some photographs of who is floating in and out and who has sunk to the bottom, we shall find that the sand is largely made up of people who are unskilled. A count of all the blue-collar men at work in the United

Kingdom reveals that those labelled 'unskilled' by the statisticians are fewer than one in twelve of the total. Yet of blue-collar males on the dole, one in three are unskilled. The higher proportion of unskilled people in the pool reflects the difficulty they have in finding a way out. The skilled are more fortunate. They generally go for a comparatively short dip before finding alternative work.

The best way to help the unskilled get out of the pool, many people say, is to train them in skills which companies need. This obviously makes sense, especially in Britain where skill shortages have been a chronic problem for years. In 1981, West Germany produced 3.5 times as many building craftsmen per person at work as did Britain, 2.5 times as many electricians, and twice as many mechanical fitters. This was an important reason why West Germany was 100 per cent more efficient than Britain in the construction industry, and 50 per cent up in manufacturing.

It is not difficult to see how persistent skill shortages can have a devastating effect on industry. Lack of skills to install, run and maintain advanced machinery slows the investment which will create wealth and, in turn, jobs. Some people believe that this is the basic problem, but it goes deeper than that. Skill shortages encourage inflexible patterns of work. Yet virtually everyone agrees that a willingness to change is vital if the economy is to produce enough jobs – and wealth – to beat unemployment.

Imagine a company with plenty of skilled maintenance staff. The most effective way to deploy them would be to spread them along the production line so that they could correct faults straight away. When the line runs smoothly they could either work on preventive maintenance (stopping trouble before it happens) or help with the production itself. They would be free to do a wide variety of jobs as the need arose.

Now imagine that the same company has much fewer maintenance employees. It would be unrealistic to disperse electricians and others along the production line because each person would have to cover an impossibly wide area. The maintenance work will have to be done by teams of trouble-shooters moving to points where the line has broken down.

But with fewer qualified staff there will be less time for preventive maintenance. Breakdowns may occur more often – so stretching the resources of the maintenance teams still further. Or the management may have to pay overtime to get the preventive work done outside normal hours, which will raise costs. Because management will want to make the most of the few skills available, it will encourage employees to concentrate on using their particular expertise rather than helping from time to time with jobs in other areas. This in turn will produce a strong demarcation of work between those of different skills. Each person will be specializing in what he or she is best at. The employees will not have the experience of working more flexibly in a variety of tasks.

It has long been known that Britain suffers from inflexible attitudes at work. Employees are frequently reluctant to shift from one type of work to another. Management may introduce a new machine which will revolutionize production, only to find that employees refuse to operate it. This is often blamed on the unions, who are accused of negative attitudes which obstruct change. But the problem is more complicated. A major factor is the long history of skill shortages which has forced workers to over-specialize in one task. If employees have only known the rigid demarcation of jobs, then it is not surprising that they hold inflexible attitudes, unreceptive to change.

Basic technical training for the unskilled who are out of work would ease some of these pressures. It would lead to more skilled labour, paving the way for more flexible patterns of work, with the result that there would be greater efficiency, more profits, more investment, more factories, and so more jobs, which would cut unemployment. People who are seen as part of one problem could become the solution to another. It sounds nice and easy – but it is not the whole story.

Take Joe. He left school (he thinks) at the age of fifteen. He never got any qualifications. Though he hardly admits it, he has difficulty in reading. He cannot concentrate either. He had held his recent job as a hospital porter for fifteen years. It had been an ideal job, apart from the pay. It required few skills, the people were friendly and Joe got on well with his mates. The only trouble had been that the hospital was one of those small ones which had been threatened with closure for years. Then it happened. Joe was out of a job.

Glib talk of training the unemployed for the skills of the future brings little comfort to Joe. Engineering skills are far too sophisticated. The world of electronics is on a different planet altogether. True, expansion of the service sector has brought a growing demand for people with person-to-person skills in various forms of customer service such as hairdressing, waiting, and sales of all kinds. There may be a chance for modest retraining here. But a good hospital porter does not necessarily make a good waiter. The adjustment will be considerable. And it may be particularly difficult for someone like Joe who lacks self-confidence and is convinced that he would be no good at anything except being a porter.

This is not to say that retraining the unemployed is out. Of course it is vital that where possible they should be taught skills, at a level with which they can cope, for jobs which will exist in the future. But it is easy to underestimate the substantial problems involved and to exaggerate what can be done.

Many jobless people, like Joe, have little self-confidence. Having done badly in exams and settled for a second-rate job, they do not expect to achieve very much. Often they feel failures. They may have had difficulty in holding down a job, or have been rejected by one employer after another. Past failures have sapped their incentive to try something new. 'Why should this make a difference when so many other things haven't?' they think. Or they may look down their street and see that the majority are out of work with scarcely a job, skilled or unskilled, to apply for. 'Why bother?' is a natural reaction. Recognizing such attitudes will dispel simplistic notions about training. Crucial though it is, training is not the easy panacea for unemployment that many suppose.

The old

Another group in the sand is the old. Though they are three times less likely than the young to become unemployed, once they are in the pool they find it almost impossible to get out. 'Well let's face it,' said fifty-five-year-old Geoff, 'if you're going to buy a horse and you've got the choice of a four-year-old and a ten-year-old to go racing with, what would you say? You'd buy the four-year-old – you wouldn't buy the ten-year-old. He's ready for the knacker's yard. You've gotta have young people in work. But at the same time, what are you going to do with your older people? They've got to have reasonable money to live on.' Two-thirds of the elderly in Britain, some 5 million people, were living in or on the margin of poverty in the late 1970s.

Geoff feels acutely the stigma of being means-tested for supplementary benefit. He wishes he could be out of it – on a pension. He would then be on a fixed amount every week with no questions asked. It is a terrible thing for Geoff to find that at the end of his working life he has to go cap-in-hand and beg the state (so it seems) for money. Normally he could expect the period before retirement to be a time of relative comfort. With the children gone from home, there would be fewer financial demands.

Perhaps Geoff had plans for spending the extra, but now all he has left is a sense of utter failure. He is at the age when many people look back over their lives, asking how meaningful their life has been and how much they have achieved. For Geoff the answer must be agony. In financial terms – the most popular yardstick of success – he has achieved nothing. He can't even afford to look after his wife.

There are of course many who welcome early retirement. It can be an opportunity to change direction, to make the most of family and home while one is still fit. Or for those who are feeling the pace of life, it can be a chance to slow down. Increasingly it is recognized that a single age of retirement can never suit everyone. Some may want to quit work in their late fifties, others in their early sixties. There is much to be said for the idea of flexible retirement, whereby people could opt to retire on a pension at any age between (say) fifty-five and sixty-five. Those who wanted to retire early could then do so. It would be a way of replacing older employees who do not want to work with unemployed people who do.

Geoff is typical of many older workers. Given the chance, he would prefer to ease himself into retirement, working part-time for a while before retiring full-time. This would avoid the painful break between being at work all day on Friday and not at all the next Monday, and it would give Geoff time to adjust to a new life. Geoff would get used to longer periods of leisure and a lower income before he finally retired. If Geoff was employed half-time, work could perhaps be shuffled around his company so that an unemployed person was recruited on a part-time basis. This might not be as good as a full-time job for those out of work, but at least it would be better than no job. It is not difficult to see how voluntary early retirement and phased retirement could make sense for both the employed and unemployed. Older workers might opt for early retirement or phased retirement, or a combination of the two. The question is how to make this a reality.

Ethnic minorities
Unemployment is far higher among ethnic minorities than the general population. Someone born in Britain and under thirty is twice as likely to be out of work if his skin is coloured than if it is not. Some people think that ethnic minorities are at a disadvantage in the job hunt because they have difficulty adjusting to a new culture, have low educational achievements and have less commitment to work.

But this is easily exaggerated. Asians, for example, seem to perform rather better at school than whites from equivalent backgrounds, but are more likely to be jobless. Surveys have shown that young West Indians are more persistent in seeking jobs than whites with similar qualifications, but have less success. A more important reason for high unemployment among ethnic minorities are company recruiting policies. 'I feel fed up,' said Jamie, an eighteen-year-old West Indian in Birmingham. 'They give the job to the white people and not the black ones. I phoned up a firm about a job and I was talking to the guy for about five minutes, and then he said, "Are you black?" And I said "What's that got to do with it?" and he put the phone down. It's happened like this to all my friends too.'

The employer at the other end of the phone may have been under considerable pressure himself. In his factory the shop floor expected the company to recruit the sons and daughters of those who already worked in the factory. To give preference to a West Indian would set the cat among the pigeons, the last thing the company could afford. Management was desperately trying to persuade the shop floor to work machines more flexibly. A large investment programme depended on this. The company needed all the goodwill it could get. It would be daft to upset the apple cart now by changing a long-standing custom.

The trouble from Jamie's point of view was that he had little chance of being hired by any other employer in the area. They all faced similar pressures. Jamie had taken the right subjects at school and achieved minimal formal qualifications for an apprenticeship. On leaving school he had sought jobs through the Careers Service, but had quickly discovered that this avenue was largely shunned by employers. They preferred informal recruitment by long-established contacts. They tended to recruit from areas where blacks were less numerous, yielded to the racial prejudices of the existing workforce, and favoured the 'lads of the dads' to 'outsiders'.

It was not that the managers were particularly prejudiced themselves. A number would have been delighted to open up their recruitment policies, but the pressures stacked against them were too great. This suggests that voluntary efforts alone will not improve the situation, despite the faith some people place in such efforts, because the obstacles are too great to expect people to overcome them on their own.

Nor is it enough to launch 'special' or remedial programmes to counter the supposed cultural or personal disadvantages of minority groups. Often this type of help is seen as *the* solution. But however well intended, special training or extra education are liable to be seen by minorities not as an opportunity to increase their chances of finding work, but as an excuse to avoid tackling the main reasons for their lack of jobs. 'It's not my fault I ain't got a job,' Jamie had said. 'It's them bleedin' employers. They don't give us a chance. People think it is us who need help, but it's the bosses that need sortin' out. I mean, what do you do if you've got all the qualifications and they still don't give you a job?'

Clearly, the ideal would be for employers in areas of ethnic diversity to recruit more racially balanced workforces. Perhaps government should compel employers to ensure that the racial composition of their employees broadly reflects the ethnic mix of the surrounding area. This of course would raise immense problems – not least the danger of a white backlash. Whites might resent what they (unjustly) saw as special treatment for minorities. Employers would also be likely to find it difficult to recruit minorities with appropriate skills. There would certainly not be enough blacks with higher qualifications to ensure that work forces were racially balanced at every level of skill. Is there no way of overcoming these problems, however, so that we can move more rapidly towards the ideal?

High unemployment spots

Besides the unskilled, the old and ethnic minorities (as well as the disabled, another very important group), the sand also contains the unemployed who live in areas particularly starved of jobs. Often these areas lie within a few miles of an affluent suburb. They can be found not only in inner cities, but also in newer residential suburbs where housing estates have been created but not the jobs to go with them.

The needs of these unemployment high spots are highlighted by the plight of many inner cities with their tatty old buildings, their brutally graffitied pavements and stairwells, their flats with broken-down lifts, and their upturned rubbish bags which provide food for stray dogs and add to the stench of decay.

Clusters of different ethnic groups mix to form a cultural stewpot of whites, blacks and browns. Many flats and houses are barely fit for habitation, and occupants have been known to take a single light bulb with them from room to room because of their poverty. Occasionally thoughts turn to the possibility of leaving. More often they focus on survival – on how to by-pass the electric meter or make the gas meter run backwards; on how to salvage some dignity from the debris of broken homes, shattered lives and destroyed hopes.

Communities have been corroded by the work of complex processes over many years. There has been the relentless tendency of high income earners to move to suburbs where they can buy a newly built house of their own, and for their place to be taken by people with few skills, expecting jobs with little pay. Major employers of labour have withered away. In some cases the docks have unloaded ships for the last time; in others, factories have moved out because of the lack of space, traffic congestion, high rates and the attraction of alternative locations.

A vicious circle of decline sets in. As jobs go and family incomes fall, the Edwardian terraced houses become more delapidated. The place gets a down-at-the-heels look. Anyone with the chance and with an ounce of initiative clears out, leaving behind the rump of a workforce more dispirited and less skilled than ever. The factory owners call it a day. They cannot get the quality labour they need. Another lift is given to the steady rise in unemployment, and the remaining few with skills have an even greater incentive to leave.

Factory planners never give the inner city a second thought. No skilled labour is available. Who is to stop the vandals getting to work on the bright new factory premises? Why should the problems of poor transport and the like which drove out the old factories be any different for a new one? And who wants to live in the inner city anyway? Decline seems inexorable and irreversible.

A common response is to throw money at the inner cities in the hope that it will create jobs. Tax relief and subsidies for companies operating in these areas have been tried. On the odd occasion this does some good. More often the money is not enough to offset the immense handicaps of locating there. Seldom has it stemmed or reversed the decline. There has been too little too late, as so often with government. There may in fact be a case for reversing this conventional approach. Instead of seeking to bring jobs to the inner city, why not try to bring the residents to jobs in the outer city? Could this in fact be done?

Taking people to jobs elsewhere in the city (if it was possible) instead of jobs to the people, might offer more hope than policies which have so far been pursued with a singular lack of success. Priority could then be given to making the inner city a decent place to live. With residents having a better chance to earn the cash to keep up the improvements, money currently spent on restoring the urban environment might have a far greater impact in the long term. And once the inner city starts to become more attractive, those who moved out may begin to drift back. The vicious circle of decline may turn into a virtuous spiral of success. What is needed is to give the spiral a new and more imaginative twist.

THE MURKY WATER

Our camera snapshot of the jobless pool will show that there is a deep layer of cloudy water above the thick sand at the bottom. If we were able to take a movie, we would see that some of the specks which make up the murky water are drifting down to the sand, while others are flowing out of the pool. Every now and again the water will lift part of the sand and carry it through the out-flow too. While the sand consists of people who have been out of work for a year or more, the murky water contains the short-term unemployed, many of whom will have already experienced at least one spell without work.

The recurrent unemployed

There is a big difference between those who work behind plush frontages in secure jobs with an attractive array of perks, good pensions, opportunities for promotion and trade union protection, and those working in the back streets in non-unionized, low paid jobs which lack pensions, perks, prospects, and above all, security. The first group have the prime jobs. The great hope of the majority in the second group is that one day they will have prime jobs, too. But at times of high unemployment the competition mounts. More and more people are looking for the good jobs, but fewer and fewer of those jobs seem to be around. And so there is a tendency for many to get stuck with inferior work.

Being left with 'trash' work means that you are more likely to switch jobs. Often the jobs are short-term by their very nature. A firm which depends on paying below-average wages may only be able to afford teenagers. When they reach the age at which adult rates are payable, they will then be replaced by other teenagers. Or else they quit the job themselves because they can't stand it any longer and think that perhaps this time they will find a better job. As many as one third of those who find jobs ten months after being unemployed can expect to be out of work again ten months later. Many of the unemployed have a record of frequent job changes, often reflecting the insecure or unsatisfactory nature of their previous employment.

Stephen, a twenty-four-year-old, was one such person. One day he was over the moon because he had been asked to an interview with a large engineering company. The job did not require many skills, but it was better paid than the one he had at the moment and seemed more permanent. At the interview, however, the manager kept asking him about the five jobs he had left over the previous four years. Stephen tried to explain how two of these jobs had been temporary and how 'lousy' the other three had been – in one the supervisor had been an insult to work with, another had involved washing up in a local cafe, which was hardly the gateway to success, and in all three the pay had been bad.

But the interviewer was not impressed. He had just seen another twenty-four-year-old who had held only one job since leaving school – in another large company which had been forced to make redundancies. Why risk hiring Stephen whose employment record looked so much worse? Stephen felt thoroughly downcast. 'Will I ever get a decent job?' he asked himself.

Stephen's case is a useful reminder not to exaggerate the difference between the long and short-term unemployed. Some people think that a person going through a three month spell without work is automatically much better off than someone who is unemployed for over a year. This can lead to the conclusion that help should be concentrated on the long-term unemployed. But Stephen illustrates how the short-term jobless can be caught between the devil of turning down inferior jobs (so risking unemployment for a long time) and the deep blue sea of taking a poor job which will look bad on their record. Because the person has had only 'trash' jobs with repeated bouts of unemployment in between, he or she becomes steadily less attractive to employers. In time, such people find it hard to get a job at all. Eventually they join the long-term, hard-core unemployed.

Stephen was worried that if he gave up his present, miserable job, this is exactly what would happen to him. But staying might not do much good either because the job would probably not have lasted long in any case. Clearly it is not enough for action to focus on the long-term jobless: it must also prevent people who cannot find permanent jobs from sinking to the bottom of the pool.

The young

Youth is a strong feature of those floating in and out of jobs. Though the proportion of young people out of work for a year of more has risen dramatically since 1979, the bulk of under twenty-fives are still on the dole for periods of less than a year. But there is an increasing tendency for young people to move between training schemes rather than between jobs. In Britain, the Youth Training Scheme aims to provide one year's training and work experience for all school-leavers without a job. The government plans to extend this period to two years. Without this scheme, well over half of the sixteen to eighteen-year-olds not at school or college in 1984 would have been on the dole. Despite various government schemes, however, some 1.3 million of those between sixteen and twenty-five were out of work.

For the young, a job means more than money. It is the signal for the individual, and the community, that the young person has become an adult. It represents a change in status, a degree of independence from the family and a rapid shift in how young people look at themselves. Prolonged unemployment can frustrate this transition. The young may feel that they ought to be grown up, but they cannot act like a man or woman because they do not have that status. They lack workmates, and they lack independence because they are still tied to the family by shortage of cash. It is this which helps to make unemployment so much more than the lack of a job.

The young have their ideals, their great hopes for the future. They dream of success, but find that the reality on offer is a dead-end job affording only the opportunity to play truant with the mind. Taking the job highlights the individual's desperate plight. It is a time too when the youngster jealously protects her or his reputation. A twenty-two-year-old in Dagenham describes his feelings. 'Some of my best friends say to me, "Why don't you get a job?" It makes me sick. People keep saying that. Oh yeah, I'm working down at some toilet, £20 a week! "£20 a week? You're working in a toilet?" And you say to them, "Well, it's a job. You told me to get a job…" Well, you can imagine what they'd think of me.'

In areas where unemployment has been high for some time, the question 'Why don't you get a job?' is never asked because the answer is so obvious – there are no jobs to get. It sometimes seems that young people in these areas are not too bothered by the lack of work. One woman in her twenties, long-term unemployed, explained the 'don't want to work syndrome' like this: 'Some of us say we do not want to work. It is not true, but when people only value you for the work you do you cannot admit to being unemployed because that means you are worthless. To say, "I do not want to work" asserts your own value because at least you have chosen the path you are taking.'

There is a conflict, then, between the need to take a job to express adulthood and an even stronger need to prove to your friends that you have a 'real job', that you are not not tied down in third-rate work. This is a warning against the right-wing view that lower youth wages will reduce unemployment. The right hopes that cutting wages will price the young into work, since more employers will be able to afford to hire them. It is just possible that lowering wages would create more jobs, but that many youngsters would refuse to work at low rates or would stick at the job only a few months because the low pay would be thought degrading. After all, since pay is seen as an indication of a person's worth, a low-paid job will imply that the individual is of little value. 'Pay peanuts and you'll get monkeys.' If this old adage is true, who wants to be a monkey?

Research shows how young people fear they will lose status among their peers unless they leave 'rubbish jobs' and tell employers to keep their 'slave wages'. If you reduce wages, it is likely that youngsters will only be prepared to do the job for a short time. So more people will be on the move more frequently, swelling the ranks of the short-term jobless, and unemployment will not fall by as much as expected. The answer to unemployment, surely, is not to turn a good job into a grotty one by keeping wages down, but to improve people's chances of sharing the best jobs.

Although the tendency to hop on and off the merry-go-round of temporary work largely reflects the lack of suitable jobs open to the young, it also represents an attempt to test reality, to try out the labour market, to look for ways of matching hope with opportunity. People may move from one job to another in the search for their vocation and in an attempt to discover how their ambitions can best be realized within the limits imposed on them. Taking a breather between jobs, or 'going for a walk' after three weeks at work provides the space in which people can reflect on their experience and decide on their next move. People were doing this long before unemployment soared to its present level. The difference today is that many more have to do it for longer, because the gap between hope and reality has widened so enormously.

This has important implications for employment schemes targeted at the young. Bob Taggart used to run former President Jimmy Carter's youth training programme, and has spent considerable time since examining the results. His conclusions are striking. It is extremely difficult to persuade youngsters to stay on a scheme for a whole year. School-leavers want to move around, to see what is going on and to experiment. The chance to do this should be built into youth training schemes by allowing participants to leave and rejoin, and by broadening the experiences available on the schemes.

Training should be divided into modules of recognized skills. To give trainees an incentive to progress through the modules, their cash allowance should be raised as they complete each one successfully. Qualifications should be standardized across the country, and where possible be matched with school and college qualifications. A comprehensive information system should record each person's progress so that if he or she drops out, training can be resumed later at the appropriate level. Meeting these tough criteria will ensure the best results.

Women

Marion used to work in a biscuit factory sorting custard creams from wafers. It was boring work, but at least there was a chance for a good chat and she was glad of the money. Sometimes though, she felt intensely frustrated. She wished she could get a better job – not just for the money but to do something more interesting. The novelty of sorting biscuits had worn off on day one. The trouble was that she did not have any qualifications. Many of the better jobs required an apprenticeship or some kind of training in skills which were typically male. 'Like to be a welder?' she used to joke with the girls. They were similar to many women in having a place of work which was far from equal.

Though the proportion of married women in Britain with jobs or looking for them rose from 50 to 60 per cent during the 1970s (a higher proportion than anywhere else in Europe except Scandinavia), married women are still at a great disadvantage. They are much more likely than men to have the least skilled and worst paid jobs. The drastic increase in unemployment since 1979 has made it even more difficult for women to get the better forms of work. With more people competing for the prime jobs, employers have less reason to give traditionally male occupations or training to women. If the post has always been filled by a man, why raise eyebrows – or hackles – by giving it to a woman?

Marion left her job to have a baby. She had always hoped to be taken on again when her daughter, Katy, started school, but shortly before that milestone the factory closed. She cannot claim benefit because her husband is in a well-paid job (and even if he were not she still could not claim because he would draw benefit on her behalf). Since she has not signed on for the dole she is not officially out of work, but she is every bit an unemployed person as those who have. She scans the job ads as avidly as they do; she pops down to the Job Centre every so often just as they do, and she is as frustrated without a job as they are. In 1981, 'work-hungry wives' were four times more likely than men *not* to have joined the official dole queue.

The pain of their unemployment may be hidden from those who think that married women can gracefully retire into a domestic role. Marion could of course do this. Spinning out her chores at home could help to fill the day. But she would remain deeply dissatisfied because she wants to be more than a housewife. She knows that even if it was completely satisfactory, the mothering role can only be temporary. The time will come when Katy will leave home.

A forty-year-old who has been a full-time housewife for a number of years may find unemployment after a short spell in paid work especially painful. That short period in a job may have been a time of hard struggle to find a new role, to swap her housewife identity for a work one. Perhaps the struggle was unsupported by the family. Then the job disappears, and she fears she is back where she began. She may be frightened that she has lost not just a job, but a battle.

Yet although women are at a disadvantage in work and can be scarred by the pain of unemployment, they fare marginally better than men in getting *some* form of work. The proportion of those able to get a job who actively wanted one in 1981 was slightly higher for women than men. Marion found a baby-minding job three mornings a week for several months. Now there is a possibility of working five mornings a week in a launderette.

There has been a mini-explosion of part-time work in Britain despite the climb in unemployment. In 1983/84 nearly 250,000 extra jobs were created. 213,000 of these were part-time, filled mainly by women. Men hardly got a look-in. But often these part-time jobs are not permanent, so that if women find work, they are quite likely to return to the murky water of unemployment. Marion may well experience recurrent spells of part-time work followed by no work at all. If women do get a permanent job, it is likely that the best opportunities will have gone to the men. It seems to be a case of jobs for the boys if you are in work, and part-time jobs for the girls if you are not.

Help for women, therefore, should focus on improving their access to prime jobs so that more options are open to them. They should have the choice of quality work, whether part or full-time. Women need the chance and encouragement to train in traditionally male skills. More positive attitudes to equal training and work opportunities for women should be fostered at school, in the workplace and by employers. Women must overcome not just an unemployment problem, but an employment one too.

CLEAR WATER

As well as sand and murky water in the jobless pool, there is a thin layer of clear water. It contains those for whom unemployment is a pleasant and often voluntary experience. It includes twenty-one-year-old Chris, for example, who was described by the interviewer as having a gorgeous tan. 'It doesn't bother me about being on the dole. Well, in the summer anyway, I go and play tennis all day, go down to the beach. Up until last year I had the caravan, so I used to go away all the time. Never bothers me,' said Chris. His experience is far from typical, but it does show that the level of unemployment is not necessarily an index of misery.

HOW LARGE IS THE POOL?

But what is the level of unemployment? How many are there in the pool? This is a matter of great debate. In October 1984 3,225,000 were officially out of work in Britain. Few take this figure at face value. Some say that the real level of unemployment is much less – as low as 2,168,000. Others would put the figure far higher, at 4,669,000. The cynic will see this as irrefutable proof that statistics can be made to show anything. For the statistical buff though, who wants to know more, the table over the page shows how these totally different conclusions can be reached. In a sense, to debate the total or percentage out of work is irrelevant, as Harold Wilson once pointed out. For the individual, unemployment is 100 per cent.

The debate over figures does highlight how very different definitions of unemployment are possible. It is important to be clear what we mean. For example, the official definition, which is used for statistical purposes, sees unemployment as comprising all those looking for work and claiming benefit. This is woefully inadequate. We have already come across Marion, who would like a job but is not entitled to benefit because her husband is working (and even if he was not, would be claiming benefit himself to cover both their needs). On what grounds is she to be excluded from the unemployed?

To cut a long debate short, a definition which does justice to what is happening on the ground is simply: 'An unemployed person is someone without a job who would want to work if they thought they could get a job.' This might seem a little curious. Why

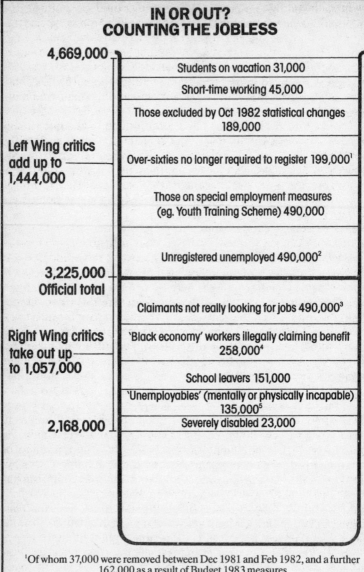

IN OR OUT?
COUNTING THE JOBLESS

4,669,000

Students on vacation 31,000

Short-time working 45,000

Those excluded by Oct 1982 statistical changes 189,000

Left Wing critics add up to 1,444,000

Over-sixties no longer required to register 199,000[1]

Those on special employment measures (eg. Youth Training Scheme) 490,000

Unregistered unemployed 490,000[2]

3,225,000 Official total

Claimants not really looking for jobs 490,000[3]

Right Wing critics take out up to 1,057,000

'Black economy' workers illegally claiming benefit 258,000[4]

School leavers 151,000

'Unemployables' (mentally or physically incapable) 135,000[5]

2,168,000

Severely disabled 23,000

[1]Of whom 37,000 were removed between Dec 1981 and Feb 1982, and a further 162,000 as a result of Budget 1983 measures
[2]Estimate based on DOE Survey 1981
[3]Estimate based on Labour Force Survey 1981
[4]Estimate based on government survey suggesting 8% of claims not justified
[5]DOE estimate

Source: *of other figures, DOE Press Notice, Nov 1984*

include the phrase, 'if they thought they could get a job'? The reason is that some people are so discouraged by job prospects that they give up hope of working again, and stop looking. But the fact that a person is discouraged from looking for work does not mean he is no longer unemployed. If a married woman was asked if she was out of work, she might well reply, 'No, I'm a housewife.' But if she thought there was a chance of finding a job, she might be out looking for it.

That is one reason why the creation of jobs does not cut the official unemployment total by the amount predicted. The government claims that hundreds of thousands of extra jobs are being created each year, yet the headline figure still climbs remorselessly. What is happening is that as more jobs come on to the market, more people start looking for them – a tale of the unexpected joining the dole queue.

Our extremely broad definition obviously commits us to a high figure for all those without jobs. We shall want to include most of those excluded by the right, as well as most of those added on by the left. For 1985 we shall be talking of a total in Britain of somewhere between 4 and 4.5 million. From the government's standpoint, this definition is most inconvenient. If it wants to lower unemployment, it is much cheaper to try to find jobs for those who claim benefit than for all who are considered unemployed in the wider definition. If a job scheme is directed at those on benefit, then the government can deduct from the cost of the scheme savings in benefit payment.

Priorities

Now there is a dilemma here. On the wider definition of unemployment we should be concerned about all those who would want to work if they thought they could get a job, regardless of whether they are claiming benefit – an expensive approach. Yet there is not exactly a super-abundance of cash for tackling unemployment. We must be realistic. To assist as many people as possible, at first we may be forced to concentrate help on those drawing benefit because it will be cheaper. But if we do this, we shall need plenty of people to protest on behalf of those whose cause is equally deserving but who have been left out because they do not receive benefit. Society needs constant prodding to do more. It needs reminding of our ultimate aim: if the unemployed count, we should count them all in.

How to decide which of those on benefit should have priority may seem an even more difficult task. With the exception of the few who positively enjoy unemployment, it would seem that all groups should be a priority! Yet shortage of cash forces those who want to do something about the problem – whether government or voluntary groups – to make painful decisions. Is there any basis on which they can choose which groups to spend their money on? Can they make a value judgment? Surely it is worse to be out of work for a year than for five weeks. The chance of getting a job lessens and despair increases the longer a person is unemployed. So should we not gear unemployment measures towards the long-term jobless?

This could be done by saying that certain schemes are only for those out of work for twelve months or more (which already happens in one or two cases). Or (as again happens to a limited extent) measures could be directed at high unemployment spots where the reduction of the working class to an out-of-work class is most marked. It is there that the long-term unemployed are concentrated, that the least skilled are most likely to live, that the old have the greatest chance of being made redundant, that ethnic minorities tend to congregate, that the short-term unemployed will most probably join the hard-core jobless and that the young still have greatest difficulty in finding work. Focusing support on unemployment high spots is the one best way to reach those with the most compelling cases, though within these areas action will still have to be targeted at particular groups.

CONCLUSION

We have not had time to look at all the groups of jobless – at the disabled, or those with dependent children, for example. Yet we have seen enough to recognize that there are major differences among the unemployed in how long they have been in the pool, their chances of getting out and how they feel about the swim. Action on unemployment will be effective only if it is sensitive to the varying needs of job-seekers. There are differing needs of the groups in the sand – the unskilled, the old, ethnic minorities and people in high unemployment spots; of groups in the murky water, notably among women and the young; and of the unemployed in clear water. Each of their particular concerns should be catered for.

Yet what appears most sharply in the photographs of the unemployment pool? Is it the pain of the individuals involved? Is it the different experiences and needs of the various groups of unemployed? Is it that the pool seems so much larger than official figures suggest? Or is it perhaps – on top of all these – the fact that the burden of being jobless is carried not by those with the broadest shoulders, but by those whose backs have already been broken? For that is what the picture shows. It is the most vulnerable and powerless members of society who are most likely to be out of work – the unskilled, the old who can only look forward to inadequate pensions, the young with the lowest educational achievements and the ethnic minorities who feel that the dice is loaded heavily against them in housing, jobs and social advancement generally.

Frequently these groups are shut away, conveniently out of sight of the rest of society, in areas where deprivation feeds off deprivation and where there is the least access to the best health care, reasonable housing and other ingredients of the good life. Unemployment adds to the existing injustice without the rest of the community having to see the results. Yet another weight falls on those who have already been asked to carry the most. The bruised get a further beating.

CHAPTER 3

Why So Many Out of Work?

People are often perplexed by the high level of unemployment. They can see plenty of tasks that need doing – mothers need child-minders, schools need teachers, buses need drivers and houses need building. Some 35 million people in the advanced industrialized countries are without jobs and want to work. So why cannot more be done to match job-seekers to the work which needs doing? Answers often get bogged down in terms like 'money supply', 'demand management' and 'structural unemployment' – notions which are clear to the expert but intimidating to the layperson. Are the secrets of unemployment to be closed to all but high-flying economists?

In this chapter we shall concentrate on four explanations of unemployment. They are not the only ones, but they have been very influential. They can be described as cash, crush, change and conflict. Cash stands for the monetarist view that a great deal of today's unemployment stems from the 1970s when there was too much money in the economy; crush is the Keynesian view that unemployment is due to the government squeezing the economy too tightly; change describes the structuralist belief that unemployment comes from shifts in the industrial foundations of the economy, and conflict focuses on class struggle as the main cause.

THE CASH ACCOUNT
A tourist port picture

The monetarist view of unemployment reminds me of a spectacle I regularly observed when, for a delightfully exotic six months of my life, I lived in Suva, the tiny capital of Fiji. Every week or so a cruise ship would dock so that its passengers (replete with travellers' cheques) could visit the famous duty-free shops. The shop-keepers, knowing that there was a quick buck to be made, would respond by promptly raising their prices, while the local residents reacted by keeping as far away as possible. As soon as the tourists' money disappeared, prices would fall and the local residents would appear once more on the streets. Monetarists would say that this is typical of how a market economy works. If money pours into the economy as it did when the tourists streamed into Suva, and there is no matching increase in what can be bought with this extra money, then prices will rise.

Now what would happen if Suva were suddenly to become a major tourist attraction and a cruise ship were to dock every day instead of once a week? Money would pour into the town and shop-keepers would put up their prices, just as before. But prices would now remain high because as one ship left, another would immediately arrive. Indeed, if more and more tourists were to spend cash in Suva – if two ships were to berth daily instead of one – the shop-keepers would be able to raise their prices still higher. Budding entrepreneurs might get in on the act by opening new shops to cater for the expanding tourist trade. This would create jobs in the shops and cafés, among local producers of art and crafts, and in firms specializing in the imports of duty-free goods.

No doubt this would delight the Fiji government, but ministers might be worried by the spiralling prices. Local residents, on lower incomes than visitors from Australia, New Zealand and Japan, would not be able to afford the 'tourist' prices. They would demand that something be done. Imagine that in response the government declared that the whole thing had got out of hand, clamped down on the tourist trade and restricted the number of visiting ships to one a week. Faced with a sharp drop in business, the shop-keepers would lower their prices to entice back the local residents. However, with less money to spend, the cafés and other shops which had flourished when business was brisk would begin to close. Their owners and employees would lose their jobs. Unemployment would return to what is technically know as its natural rate, which is the level it had been before the extra tourists arrived – its level when the economy had been jogging along normally.

This illustrates how monetarists see unemployment arising in a modern society. Governments, they say, try to keep down unemployment by pouring money into their economies. The classic case of this in many countries occurred in the early and late 1970s when lots of new money was created, only to be followed by a steep rise in prices. Although it seemed that it was the jump in oil prices which sparked off inflation, in fact (say the monetarists) the higher oil prices were only made possible by the amount of money already floating around the world. If there had been less money in circulation, the West would not have been in a position to pay so much for oil, and the Arabs would have been unable to raise prices by such a large amount.

The inflation produced by these money-booms was intolerable, not least because pensioners and others on fixed incomes found themselves in the same position as the Suva residents: they could not afford the higher prices. So governments cut back the amount of new money entering their economies which meant that individuals and companies had less to spend. Parts of factories, sometimes whole plants, had to close and unemployment soared. According to the monetarists then, abnormally high unemployment is the result of efforts to bring the money supply (and hence inflation) back under control. Once inflation returns to an acceptable level, unemployment will settle down to its natural rate.

Competition

This of course leaves the question: what happens if a country manages to control inflation but still has high unemployment? The monetarist answer stresses the role of competition. If there is plenty of competition, the economy will work more efficiently. And an efficient economy gives rise to jobs. If a state company were to monopolize Suva's duty-free trade, for example, monetarists would expect all sorts of inefficiency to creep in. There would be none of the price cutting by competitors to spur on the company to seek ways of lowering its prices – perhaps by buying its merchandize from cheaper suppliers, or keeping down wages or reducing the number of staff.

Duty-free goods would be more expensive, which means that tourists would buy less of them. Perhaps Suva would get the reputation of being not a particularly cheap place to visit. Fewer ships would dock, sales would fall, staff would have to be laid off and unemployment would rise. Suva would end up with a higher natural rate of unemployment than if plenty of store-keepers were competing against each other.

So for the monetarist, unemployment can be unnatural because there is too much money, or natural because there is too little competition. Until recently in the West, the stress has been on controlling the money supply to avoid inflation which produces unemployment. Hence the term 'monetarist'. Now that the money-supply battle has been largely won, however, attention has shifted to the lack of competition.

In the United Kingdom, monetarists say, competition is weak partly because there are not enough small firms competing with the powerful big ones. Therefore, everything possible must be done to encourage small businesses. A more important problem is that there is not enough competition in the labour market. If lots of people are seeking work, wages should fall. Smaller pay packets would reduce company costs, enabling firms to sell more goods abroad (or beat off imports), expand operations and recruit the unemployed. But trade union power prevents this happening. What we need is to allow the wages of some people to fall, like those paid to teenagers, and to stand up to the unions so that competitive forces cut pay rises in general. More competition plus tight control of the money-supply is the recipe for jobs.

A false picture?

The monetarist view is helpful because it underlines the way that competition can generate efficiency which can create jobs. It also highlights the very obvious point that unemployment cannot be solved by throwing money at it. Pouring money into the economy in the hope that it will finance the creation of jobs would risk refuelling inflation. It could have a similar effect to increasing the flow of tourist money into Suva. That is one reason why it is not as easy a task as some believe to put the unemployed to work in jobs which clearly need doing.

On the other hand, critics point to the difficulty monetarists have in deciding what the money supply actually is. Does it include only currency notes and bank deposits, or building society deposits as well? Imagine that a group of scientists were to say that a particular experiment depended on having precisely the right amount of air. We would not be very impressed if we found out that some of the scientists were saying that by air they meant oxygen, while others mean oxygen and nitrogen. We might well feel that such imprecision cast considerable doubt on the conclusions drawn from the experiment. Likewise, say the critics, monetarists seem so unsure about what to include in the money supply that their economic theory should be received with similar scepticism.

Furthermore, the critics continue, modern economies are not as simple as our tourist port. In Suva the cruise ships arrived, and the shop-keepers made their response which was to raise prices. The order was first the tourists (bringing a rise in the supply of money), and second the increase in prices. A look at the facts, say many economists, shows that modern societies work very differently. Instead of the money-supply chicken coming before the inflationary egg, it is the other way round. First prices rise; next the money supply goes up to 'accommodate' inflation. So rather than the supply of money spurting up before the 1973 oil shock, as

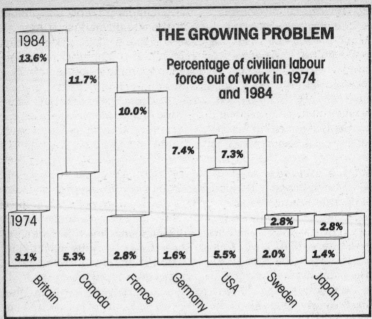

THE GROWING PROBLEM

Percentage of civilian labour force out of work in 1974 and 1984

1984
13.6%
11.7%
10.0%
7.4% 7.3%
2.8% 2.8%

1974
3.1% 5.3% 2.8% 1.6% 5.5% 2.0% 1.4%

Britain Canada France Germany USA Sweden Japan

Source: US Bureau of Labor

monetarists claim, what happened was that the oil shock came first. Then the money supply went up so that people could pay for the more expensive oil. To understand inflation, therefore, you should look not at changes in the amount of money in circulation, but at the social and political behaviour which produced those changes.

In the same way, to understand unemployment it is no good saying, 'Look, the supply of money is growing less fast. That is why unemployment has started to rise.' It may just be that the money supply is increasing less rapidly *because* unemployment has begun to rise. If you think of it in terms of a household, it is not less money coming into the family which puts the father out of work. It is the father losing his job (his behaviour in the 'real' economy) which leads to a drop in income.

Critics also claim that monetarists place too much faith in competition. Businessmen often pursue immediate goals at the cost of the economy's long-term health. They can be so keen to make a quick profit, for example, that they skimp on training tomorrow's workforce. There is a strong temptation to free-ride on other firms' training efforts and poach when necessary. If too many companies do this, there will not be enough skilled labour to work all the new factories needed to cut unemployment. Government action may therefore be required to ensure that sufficient training takes place. This points strongly to the fact that there can be important reasons apart from the lack of competition for a high level of natural unemployment. Indeed, competition itself can be a problem!

Added to this, the attempt to check pay rises by more competition, in the hope that this will create jobs, is almost certainly doomed because of the herculean difficulties involved. If employees see orders pouring into the factory, they know management will be in a weak position to resist a strike. They know it can make more sense for a company to give in to the workforce and meet those orders than to lose customers because of industrial action. 'Why not make a profit today while the going is good?' the boss will think. 'The chance may be gone tomorrow.' If orders are slack, on the other hand, employees know there is a risk of being laid off. They are likely to give way to management more easily. As the economy recovers and orders pick up, we can expect the balance of power to shift towards the shop floor.

Management has its own reasons for allowing wages to rise, quite apart from trade union power. If self-esteem is linked to pay (the more I'm paid the better I feel), then keeping pay below what the shop-floor thinks is reasonable is likely to demoralize employees. The workforce will feel badly treated, motivation will drop and the quantity and quality of work will decline. No self-respecting manager wants to work in an environment like that. What the best companies strive for is a highly paid, highly motivated and highly efficient workforce. They don't always get it, but the ideal is far more attractive than managing low-paid, disgruntled and can't-be-bothered employees.

In short, any attempt to dampen wage rises is likely to be caught in a pincer movement from the trade unions on one side and employers on the other. Anti-union laws, holding down public service pay, cutting youth wages, encouraging people to take low paid jobs and other right-wing techniques to slow the rise in wages will have some effect. But given the strength of the pincer movement, they are not likely to slice unemployment dramatically.

Summary chart: Monetarist

Problem Government pours money into the economy. Prices rise. People can't pay. Government cuts back growth of money, production falls, and unemployment rises above its natural rate. Not enough competition increases natural rate.

Solution Control of money supply will avoid the inflation which eventually leads to unemployment.
More competition will reduce natural unemployment.

Critical questions What is 'money'?
Does the money supply govern the rest of the economy, or vice versa?
How big a cause of natural unemployment is the lack of competition?
Will efforts to increase labour competition create many jobs?

THE CRUSH VIEW

A second explanation for unemployment is put forward by the Keynesian school of economists, who take their name from the pioneering British economist of the inter-war years, John Maynard Keynes. The basic difference between the Keynesian and the monetarist views is that the monetarists focus on the amount of money in circulation, whereas the Keynesians are more interested in what is happening in the 'real' economy – in the behaviour of people as they buy and sell goods, fix wages, and so on. It is this behaviour which determines the supply of money, they say, not the other way round. We can illustrate this from Britain, remembering that other countries will have had different experiences.

It was not an expansion of the money supply, but the doubling of oil prices plus a pay explosion which led to the prices surge of 1979/80. This made some squeeze of the economy necessary to force out inflation. The squeeze was accomplished largely by pushing people out of work, much as water is forced out of a squeezy mop. The government squeezed the economy not (as it thought it was doing) by reining in the supply of money, but by building less houses, fewer roads and so on. Those who would have been employed in this construction work (and other forms of government employment) lost their jobs, along with workers in companies supplying construction materials. The government also raised interest rates, which made it more difficult for businesses to create jobs by borrowing money for new projects. As the number out of work grew, the pressure for wage increases to out-do the rise in prices was reduced. If your mate loses his job, you are unlikely to risk your own by striking for higher pay.

With fewer people in jobs and with those in work taking lower pay increases, less money was needed to pay Britain's shrinking workforce. So the supply of money increased less rapidly. But notice the order. Instead of a more tightly controlled money supply leading to unemployment, it was the rise in unemployment (and other events in the 'real' economy) which cut back the growth of the money supply.

Easing the squeeze

The trouble according to the Keynesians is that the mop was squeezed too tightly. Too many people were forced out of work. Particularly in the early days (1979-81) the government went for overkill on inflation. It did not make enough allowance for the impact of North Sea oil. As the oil came on stream, Britain's energy imports fell sharply. The result was that the value of what Britain sold abroad leapt ahead of what she bought from the rest of the world. With more wealth pouring into the country than flowing out, Britain looked a good place to invest in. So people overseas bought pounds, and the more they bought, the more the pound's value soared against the dollar.

Unfortunately, though, the muscular pound became too strong, so that British companies found it increasingly difficult to export their goods. Instead of a £100 product being worth 200 dollars, at one point it might have sold for as much as 240 dollars – which meant that fewer people would have wanted to buy it. Able to sell less, the manufacturer would have had to lay people off, or close down completely. One reason why exporters found it difficult to take advantage of the *falling* pound in 1984/85 was that the rising pound of the previous years had forced many factories to close.

The government made the situation worse by refusing to spend more itself. Increased spending on schools, hospitals, houses and the like would have brought more jobs into existence. Or reducing interest rates would have enabled companies to expand their operations, producing still more jobs. Both of these measures would have created jobs and stemmed the rise in the value of the pound. Imports would have been sucked in as those who found employment spent some of their pay on goods from abroad. This would have reduced the enormous surplus on Britain's trade, and made the country less attractive to foreign visitors, who would have then bought fewer pounds. The rise in sterling's value would have been checked, so that what sold for 240 dollars might have sold for 210 dollars instead. As a result, companies would have had to make less people redundant and a few might have been able actually to create jobs (to add to those already produced by higher government spending and lower interest rates).

Keynesians believe that the government could have squeezed the mop more gently, and still have defeated inflation. By making the recession too savage, it pushed unemployment higher than it need have done. The operation cured inflation, but left the patient half dead.

How much can the mop absorb?

There is a catch, however. A squeezy mop can only absorb so much water. If you want it to absorb more, the sponge has to be made more porous, otherwise it will become saturated too quickly. The same can happen with the economy. It can become saturated, by absorbing too many of the unemployed, if it grows too fast. The economy then has to be squeezed again to get rid of the excess people in the workforce, so that once more unemployment starts to rise.

One reason why the economy can become saturated is known in the trade as 'supply bottlenecks'. Imagine a town where the main construction companies receive a flood of new orders in the space of a month. The first thing they will do is to order additional supplies of cement, bricks, timber and the like. If lots of these orders are placed close together, the suppliers may find that they cannot meet the extra demand. Astute businessmen that they are, they may well react by putting up their prices to take advantage of the situation. Some construction companies will be able to get their orders at the higher prices and start work, but others will have to wait because of the shortages.

The construction firms will also need skilled labour, but that may be in short supply for similar reasons. People cannot become trained overnight to meet an unexpected surge in the demand for skills. Those skilled workers who are available are likely to be as canny as the suppliers of building materials. They will raise their prices, too. Up will go their wages. So again, some companies will be able to hire the labour they require but at higher wages; others, less fortunate, will experience shortages and delays in completing their contracts.

This illustrates the point, say the Keynesians, that although the government has throttled the economy and made unemployment higher that it need have been, the scope for relaxing the squeeze is limited. If the government eases the mop too fast, the economy will become saturated because the sponge is not porous enough to absorb all the unemployed. Firms up and down the country would be unable to buy the supplies they need, and would turn to overseas suppliers instead. Jobs would be created outside the country rather then inside.

Not only would too rapid growth be checked by shortages of materials, equipment and skilled labour, but it could be choked to death if suppliers and skilled labourers exploit the shortages by raising prices and wages. A ricochet effect on other wages and prices would make the country's goods more expensive than those produced elsewhere. If the price of British Leyland cars went up faster than foreign makes, thanks to a hike in wages, more people would soon turn to imports. British Leyland would have to respond to the fall in sales by laying workers off, increasing unemployment.

How limited the scope is for economic expansion is a matter of hot debate among Keynesians, and will vary from one country to another. Some say that the economy could become more porous, more able to absorb the jobless, if the government went for selective growth. Government should try to boost those regions where supply shortages are least likely to appear rapidly. A shove might be given to construction in an area of high unemployment by launching a major programme of house building and renovation. This would create a demand for labour and building materials which would lift other parts of the economy. Such an approach would be better than encouraging a major boom in construction throughout the economy, because in low unemployment regions supply bottlenecks would be likely to emerge quite soon, and these would jack up prices.

The approach would work particularly well, many Keynesians think, if it was accompanied by a prices and incomes policy. Government control of wages would stop unions from taking advantage of any labour shortages to bid for higher pay. Price control would prevent companies making a tide of new orders the excuse for a jump in prices. So the mop could be opened more quickly without inflation shooting up all over again.

On this view, the government has squeezed the economy unnecessarily tightly. The key word is 'unnecessarily'. For Keynesians argue that techniques like regional policy and prices and incomes policy can be used to relax the economic mop in a way that absorbs some of the unemployed without doing long-term harm. Government is largely to blame for how much unemployment has risen because it has not employed these techniques.

So instead of the monetarist preference for a hands-off approach which allows competition to get on with the job of reducing natural unemployment, the Keynesians advocate positive intervention by government to speed up the rate of growth and to prevent unrestrained competition pushing up wages and prices.

An adequate approach?

The advantage of the Keynesian view is that it underlines the importance of policies other than control of the money supply in managing the economy. However, the big question 'squeezy mop' economists have to answer is: how many of their techniques will actually work? For example, it is all very well, the critics say, to advocate a prices and incomes policy. The economist can sit in his ivory tower and make the suggestion without having to put it into practice. He can say 'wages and prices ought to be controlled' and then conveniently pass to the politician the buck of how to do it. But how do you persuade people to stick to the rules? Pay policies have not been very successful in the past. Why should they work in the future?

The idea of a tax-based incomes policy is becoming increasingly popular among advocates of pay and price controls precisely because other forms of pay restraint seem to have failed. At its simplest, under a tax-based policy government would set a maximum for pay rises – say 6 per cent. If anyone got more than that, 8 per cent for example, the extra 2 per cent would be heavily taxed. The tax could either be levied on offending employees, or on companies who paid over the odds. If workers had to pay the tax, unions might be strongly discouraged from hoisting pay above the government ceiling. If the tax fell on employers, companies would have a greater incentive to resist union demands.

The problem would be to make the policy both feasible to administer and flexible in response to business realities. The practicalities of company life would require many exceptions. Rises above the norm would be needed for those who were promoted, who ought to be paid more because their jobs had become more skilled, or who deserved to be rewarded for improved performance. Without these exceptions, people would have no incentive to change jobs and improve working practices, and this would produce all kinds of inefficiency. Pay would end up in a claustrophobic strait-jacket. Yet policing these exemptions would be a mind-boggling task – so much so that many believe it is out of the question. The choice is between a rigid policy (with just a few exceptions) and no policy at all.

It is a moot point whether the advantage of holding down pay through a rigid policy would outweigh the inefficiencies caused by the lack of flexibility. Certainly the inefficiencies would cut the extra growth made possible by pay controls, and hence the impact on jobs. Yet no incomes policy would remove the one means of checking the inflationary pay rises that a big jump in government spending could spark off. It would prevent public spending being raised – without igniting inflation – by the amount needed to radically shorten the dole queue.

Summary chart: Keynesian

Problem Government curbs inflation by cuts in public spending and higher interest rates. This squeezes people out of jobs (and leads to a smaller growth of the money supply). The squeeze has been too tight.

Supply shortages limit scope for relaxing the squeeze; may lead to inflation.

Solution Government must not attack inflation so savagely that unemployment climbs unnecessarily high.

Government should intervene positively to promote growth by more public spending, and use techniques like regional policy and prices and incomes policy to prevent supply shortages causing inflation.

Critical question Will techniques like pay and prices policy work?

THE CHANGE VIEW
Declining old industries

One of the more important buildings in Suva was destroyed by a cyclone in the early 1950s. Rumour has it that the colonial government in its wisdom decreed that the replacement should be strong enough to withstand any cyclone – except one the size that had levelled its predecessor! The structuralist view of unemployment attributes its rise to the collapse of old industries like ship building, steelmaking and textiles. They have been blown down by the wind of competition, particularly from countries in the Far East which can produce ships, steel and clothes at a fraction of European or American prices. Closure of these industries has forced their workers onto the dole.

To get the force of this view, imagine that the tenants of our Suva building were to discover that it was highly vulnerable to cyclones. They would be unlikely to pore over their rent books, check how much rent they had paid and leave it at that. Just as these flows of cash would not be of much relevance to their problem, so, it is said, the money supply figures beloved by monetarists are scarcely relevant to what has been happening in the advanced industrial countries. The problem lies in the structure of these economies, not in the cash flowing round them.

What the tenants would be more likely to do is to phone the landlord and ask him to make the building safe. This is what has happened in effect when a government has propped up declining industries with subsidies and other kinds of support. Since this involves public spending, the Keynesian view of unemployment becomes rather more relevant than the monetarist one. Pouring money into these industries is one way for governments to ease the pressure on the mop so that fewer people are squeezed out of work.

However, on inspecting the building, the landlord might decide that it would be too expensive to strengthen it. From his point of view, it would make more sense to pull the building down and start again, but that is bad news for the tenants who find themselves without a place to live. This is precisely the conclusion governments have increasingly reached about large sections of traditional industry. It is too expensive to keep supporting them when their products cost far more than if they were made overseas. The time has come to let many of these industries collapse (or at least decline), which of course leaves their employees without a place to work.

A good example is the European steel industry. At its peak in 1970 the West European steel industry employed nearly half a million workers in more than 100 profitable corporations. By 1980 though, faced with intense competition from the Far East, only one or two of these corporations were making a profit. The rest were being kept alive by subsidies running to billions of pounds. The time had come for a painful adjustment to reality. Mills were closed and labour shed as the industry slimmed itself into shape. In the process the lives of many were ruined. New investment has seldom flowed into the old steel towns, but into localities often a long distance away. So those who lost their jobs have been given little chance of finding alternative work in areas where they have grown up, made their friends and feel they belong. They are casualties of what is described as structural unemployment.

What is decisive, on this view, are changes in the core structure of the economy. The government can control the money supply and try to improve competition, or it can increase public spending and tackle the problem of supply shortages, and this will have an effect in the short term. But what ultimately counts in understanding unemployment is what is happening to the country's basic industrial structure.

The great strength of the structuralist view is that it underscores how difficult it can be to match job-seekers to the work that needs doing. Often the new jobs are some distance from decaying industries. 'If that is the case,' people sometimes ask, 'why won't the unemployed move to where the jobs are? Is it because life on the dole, with large redundancy pay-outs, is too easy? Should we give them less dole-money so that they would have more incentive to move?'

People who think this do not realize how much it is to ask the victims of structural change, who feel vulnerable enough, to swap the safety of family and neighbourhood for the risk of the unknown. Reducing the size of the dole cheque, in fact, will probably leave the unemployed person less rather than more mobile. With smaller cash payments from the state, the jobless would be more heavily dependent on family and friends for food, housing and clothes. They would be tied still more closely to their community. Sizeable grants and help with housing can encourage people to move. But this is no easy answer. The grants have to be large enough to overcome the close-knit bonds of a community where people have lived all their lives, and there needs to be a good chance of a job at the other end. An alternative approach is to bring jobs to the people through some form of regional policy.

The big problem with the structuralist view however, is that it does not explain all the rise in unemployment. The sharpest rise in Britain's jobless has been in the West Midlands, where many light engineering companies are based. If *they* are closing down, then the problem can hardly be confined to a handful of the most traditional industries.

Declng new industries as well

This has led some to adopt a more drastic version of the 'collapsing house' view. It is not one building that is in danger of falling down, they say, but the whole street. For years, in fact, the entire neighbourhood has been in decay. Despite a variety of efforts to prop the buildings up, the walls keep crumbling. We are faced with a massive crisis. The Cambridge Economic Policy Group has pushed this as an explanation for Britain's unemployment in particular. British industry has been in decline for years, it says. As a result, the country has tended to import steadily more factory and consumer goods without a matching increase in exports. In this respect, 1983 was an historic year. Though there was an overall surplus on trade (thanks to North Sea oil), for the first time since the industrial revolution Britain imported more factory machinery and more high street wares than she exported. And she went out with a bang, not a whimper. A £15 billion surplus in manufacturing exports over imports in 1977 was turned into a deficit of over £5 billion in 1983.

The solution, says this version of the structural view, is to barricade the economy with import controls. Restricting imports would protect industry before it is destroyed by foreign competition. It would give a chance for new industries like micro-electronics to develop, while older industries would have a breathing space to modernize and adapt. Fewer imported trucks, for example, might enable British Leyland's truck division to increase sales by enough to put on a third shift. Making more trucks on existing machinery would boost profits and provide more cash for investment. Extra investment would lead to better machinery and better training for people to use the machines. This would enable BL to keep trucking by producing vehicles more cheaply and at a higher quality, which would push up sales and generate more profits, more investment, more efficiency and so on. A few such spins round the circle of growth by a number of major industries, and the economy might take off on a permanent basis. Britain would be ready to emerge from its cocoon, transformed and able to face the world, at which point import controls could be dismantled.

Blaming unemployment on the lack of import controls highlights Britain's inefficiency. She is not very good at producing enough of what people want, of a quality they demand, at a price they are willing to pay, to create jobs for all who are looking for them. Between 1970 and 1980 Britain's pay went up nearly twice as much as her main competitors, while the amount produced by each person rose by almost exactly half! No wonder companies found it increasingly difficult to compete with imports and sell their goods overseas. No wonder they did not produce the wealth that would have enabled more of those looking for jobs to be employed in the tasks that so evidently need doing. No wonder unemployment has risen.

On the other hand, many have stressed the huge practical

MORE PAY FOR LESS
Pay increases 1970-80 seen against increases in output per employee

190%

INCOME
341%

OUTPUT
27%

51%

Britain   Main overseas competitors

Source: National Institute Economic Review

difficulties in the way of import controls. They would be against Common Market rules. Other countries might retaliate. If Britain keeps out French Renaults, why should France continue to import British Metros? It is doubtful, too, whether feather-bedding industry is the best way to encourage change. Businessmen might take advantage of the extra comfort to go to sleep. 'We've got a safe home market,' they might think. 'Government will keep out the nasty imports. We don't need to work too hard at becoming more efficient.' Mammoth efforts might be required to wake them up, and it is not at all clear that government has the administrative resources to succeed. Planning agreements between government and industry, and other measures to improve efficiency suggested by left-wing believers in import controls, are unlikely to be enough. The stick of being beaten by the competition may be a more powerful incentive to modernize than the carrot of a comfortably secluded home market.

Summary chart: Structuralist

Problem Unemployment caused by closure of old industries. New firms, which could provide work for the jobless open in different areas.

Solution Bring jobs to the people by regional policy and people to the jobs by mobility policy.

Protect British industry with import controls till it is strong enough to face the world.

Critical questions How much unemployment is caused by the decline of old industries?

Will import controls provide a context for change or feather-bed industry ?

THE CONFLICT VIEW

A fourth way to look at unemployment is to see it as the outcome of a conflict between the owners of capital and the working class. A number of explanations focus on this. They owe much to the insights of Karl Marx, though they are not always Marxist themselves. One spotlights the competing loyalties of managers and employees. Typically, managers' prime commitment at work is to the company. They have a strong incentive to ally themselves to the interests of the company's shareholders because promotion is the route to higher earnings. And promotion comes by promoting the goals of the business – selling more, developing new products, and so on.

Workers' pay, on the other hand, often peaks when the individual is in his or her early 20s. After that, incomes rise only if management grants a pay increase to the workforce as a whole. This would be reason enough for employees to develop a strong loyalty to each other, as together they press for higher pay. The loyalty is reinforced, however, by the actual circumstances of work. If for most of the year you spend eight hours a day with a group of people for five days a week, you are very likely to develop friendships with them and a sense of commitment to one another.

If in addition there is a years' old tendency for decisions to be 'handed down from on high', your natural inclination will be to react defensively: 'Can I trust management?' 'Does it have my interests at heart? How can I bind with workmates to protect myself? Let's join a trade union.' The prime loyalty of employees tends to be towards the people they work with rather than the employer they work for.

Conflicts at work

Instead of the creative energies of the workforce being directed towards improving the efficiency of the business, they often focus on protecting the immediate interests of the group. An extreme case is the company which produced steel products. The workforce found that the company machines could also turn out a very marketable line of darts. So the employees set to work quietly using company material, company equipment and company time to make these darts 'on the side'. A firm within a firm grew up. The informal dart company made a healthy profit, while the official business made a thumping loss!

The management-worker divide turns industrial relations into a battlefield where the two sides struggle for advantage. Occasionally the conflict breaks into open warfare with a strike. But mostly it takes the form of a guerrilla struggle in which the two sides snipe at each other over pay and employee performance. When unemployment is low (so that management cannot replace difficult staff) the unions may gain the upper hand. Perhaps management wants to introduce a bonus system to relate pay more closely to performance. Employees may hold on to the existing flat-rate system under which everyone is paid the same regardless of effort. Or the new system is introduced, only to be sabotaged by employees who negotiate easy-to-reach output targets for which bonus is paid. Everyone knows the targets are so easy that they might as well not exist, but management dare not resist lest the workforce ban overtime or come out on strike. The cost of disruption, management thinks, will be far greater than the cost of a quick concession.

Workers may band together to win pay increases way ahead of improvements in company efficiency. Or they may resist the installation of a new machine which will threaten age-old working practices. It is not that they are being bloody-minded. Their response is entirely rational given the 'they own it, we work it' structure of business, which breeds divisive group loyalties: 'It's management's job to manage. They make the decisions. If it's a problem, it's their problem.' The result is an uncooperative spirit which saps the energies of management.

So in the case of the new machine, endless time and effort may be spent by management trying to get people to agree. Arguments that it will help the company fail to cut much ice, because that is not the union's concern. Suggestions that it will benefit the workforce may be greeted with disbelief because the decision has been taken over their heads. At last a mucky compromise is reached. The machine will be installed, but it will be worked in a traditional and inefficient way. People will have settled for second best. Yet second-best decisions day after day breed lethargy. Production staff, salespeople, researchers and managers will conclude that it is not worth making the effort. Why do your best when no one else will? Management will begin to 'muck people around' because it does not care, which will make the workforce angry and even less co-operative. The company will grow more slowly. Shareholders will get fewer profits.

Unemployment - a secret weapon

Eventually unemployment comes to the businessman's aid. What is seen as lack of labour discipline in one country encourages those with capital to invest more in countries where the workers are cheaper or more docile. Instead of building a car assembly plant in Europe, it may be located in an advanced Third World country where unemployment is higher. Unemployment (an estimated 300 million are out of work in the Third World), plus a lower standard of living will cower the labour force into accepting lower wages and a stricter work regime than in Europe. Other companies may do the same. As less investment flows into Europe, fewer jobs will be created and unemployment will rise. More and more companies with headquarters in New York, London or Tokyo are setting up branch companies in the Third World. They expect the trend to accelerate.

At the same time European governments may act, perhaps by reining in public spending, to curb the inflationary effects of an 'ill-disciplined' workforce. Whatever their political complexion, the resulting unemployment will be seen as the inevitable price of making the system work. (Although left-wing governments want to make the system fairer, they are as concerned as everyone else to see it work.) So unemployment becomes not only a means of industrial discipline in the Third World, but increasingly a way to restrain the workforce in the West.

European employees accept smaller pay increases and new working practices to save their jobs – as has happened quite dramatically since 1980. Profits pick up, and investment too, as the accumulation of European capital resumes till the next crisis arrives. Unemployment will have done its job, which is to regulate the system. It is not that businessmen are being deliberately malicious. Unemployment is just the inevitable result of breaking the rules of a system in which power and wealth are concentrated in the hands of relatively few.

Reducing conflict

Much of this would be recognized by economists who do not see society in class-conflict terms. They would agree that unemployment often moderates the so-called 'excessive' demands of trade unions. Where this view parts company from the others is in how it links industrial conflict and unemployment to class antagonism arising from the restricted ownership of capital. The focus is on the clash between capitalist and worker. To stop with monetarist, Keynesian or structuralist views of unemployment, it is said, is to miss the key dynamic of society. Capitalism will always tend towards unemployment crises because the ownership of business is separate from the workers who operate it.

There are all sorts of problems with this. For example, when many workers today own capital by joining pension plans, how great a distinction is there between capitalist and working classes? Yet you don't have to be a Marxist to see that the conflict diagnosis comes close in many ways to what actually goes on in companies and that bridging the management-worker divide would enable industry to become more efficient and create more jobs.

From across the political spectrum, therefore, have come a variety of ideas for bringing the two sides together. Some suggest co-operatives in which employees would actually own the companies where they work. Less radical is the idea of giving the workers more chance to share company profits and a greater say in how the business is run. In return, unions might be asked to limit their pay demands. A trade-off like this would free government to increase its spending on jobs, without the risk of a pay explosion causing inflation.

One problem with traditional incomes policies is that they reduced the pay-bargaining role of shop-stewards. Union officials became less important, which gave them every reason to oppose pay controls and try to undermine them. However, if shop-stewards were given more say in other decision-making aspects of business, their smaller role over pay could be offset by a larger role in management. If profit-sharing was also extended, they would have an incentive to use their new role to increase profits. Promoting efficiency, so lifting profits in which workers could share, would be a way to raise incomes despite limitations on pay. The result might be greater business efficiency, producing more growth and jobs.

The trouble is that over a century of 'them' and 'us' attitudes at work would have to be changed, and this could not be done overnight. Unions might be tempted to use their greater influence to press for short-term advantages at the cost of the firm's long-term health. They might demand a larger slice of today's profits to compensate for pay restraint, leaving less for investment tomorrow. At the same time, managers would be likely to defend strongly their traditional right to manage. This is no reason for opposing greater employee ownership of companies and more industrial democracy in some form. Both are highly desirable. But they are not likely to improve the economy by much in the short term.

Summary chart: Conflict

Problem Management-worker divide produces shop-floor conflict and downward spiral of second-best compromises. Profits fall. Unemployment restores labour discipline so that management can accumulate more capital.

Solution Let workers own their companies – say by promoting co-operatives.

Critical question   What is at the heart of society – class conflict or community of interest?

LEARNING FROM EACH VIEW

This over-simplified tour of the cash, crush, change and conflict views of unemployment underlines how complex the problem is. In a way, the picture is rather depressing. There is no simple explanation. Nor is there a set of policies, flowing from any one particular view, which appears sufficiently workable to provide an answer. Every diagnosis and every prescription seems to have at least one major disadvantage. We shall need to keep this in mind when we think of ways to tackle unemployment. It is no good being naively hopeful about what can be done. There *is* reason to hope, but the reason is based on imagination and realism – not exalted, head-in-the-clouds optimism.

In another way the picture is reassuring, especially for the individual out of work. Sometimes the jobless are tempted to blame themselves for their plight, to think that in some way it is their fault. Realizing how deep-seated the causes of unemployment are can come as an encouragement. They can see themselves as the victim of a problem, not the cause of it. They are free to stop accusing themselves.

Each of the explanations we have looked at goes one step further back. The monetarist, 'tourist port' view focuses on changes in the money supply. The Keynesian 'squeezy mop' account tries to get behind the money supply to what governments are doing to the 'real' economy when they raise or lower interest rates and change government spending. The 'collapsing house' explanation goes still further back to what is happening to the basic structure of industry. Others would want to probe even further behind the surface to the class conflicts which lie at the heart of industry. Each view is capable of international expansion to explain trends in the world economy.

Though none of the explanations are adequate, nor the policy ideas which flow from them, all four approaches do have something to say. The 'cash' view highlights the need to improve competition; the 'crush' view the need for more government spending without refuelling inflation; the 'change' view the vulnerability of many companies to imports, and the 'conflict' view the debilitating effects of disharmony on the shop-floor. It is better to learn from the insights of each perspective than to swallow any one whole.

Yet some people want to move beyond all this. They would say that another factor is at work, and that in time it will dwarf all these other explanations of unemployment. New technologies are producing huge changes in the nature of work. We could be faced with a perpetually large pool of unemployed people. Could it be, in fact, that the nature of the problem will change – that the causes of tomorrow's unemployment will differ from today's?

CHAPTER 4

The Future of Work

NEW TECHNOLOGIES ON THE LOOSE

In April 1984 it was reported that Rolls Royce's Osmaston Road plant in Derby had spent £4 million on an automated production line making turbine blades for its aero engines. Micro-processors, robotized handlers and advanced machine tools had been bolted together to transform an operation which used to be slow, labour-intensive and (for all the painstaking effort involved) unreliable. Three men per shift were now producing what once required thirty, and costs had been slashed by a fifth. There was still plenty of scope for increasing output, but no one was expecting this to produce jobs. The machines would simply be made to work faster and even more efficiently.

Much the same is happening in countless factories around the industrialized world. A robotic population explosion is under way, and many are profoundly worried about what it will do to jobs. But robots are only part of the immense technological change engulfing society. Four technologies have come together to produce the well-publicized information revolution: the chip, the bird, the wire and the screen, as one TV programme neatly described them.

The chip is the micro-processor that makes the tiny computer possible. The bird is the communications satellite which allows any piece of information to bounce into any corner of the globe. The wire is the telephone wire, now 100 years old, but vastly expanded by fibre optics to carry almost an infinitude of signals. And the screen is the TV.

These technologies have already started to produce the worker-less factory, such as Fujitsu Fanuc's plant in Japan, where industrial robots, controlled by mini computers, produce more industrial robots without human intervention – a case of robots breeding robots. They are beginning to produce the 'paperless office', in which memoranda, messages and designs are circulated electronically with little or no human intervention. And they will increasingly produce the almost limitless information that comes from access at work, in the home, in the car or virtually wherever the individual might be, to knowledge on an enormous scale. People will be surrounded by more information than they had ever dreamed possible.

Often the talk is of new technology (rather than new technologies) as if there was a single technology at work. But the truth is that a host of technologies are busily shaking our assumptions about what can and cannot be done. We are confronted by a technological hybrid rather than a micro-monster. Biotechnology, for example, is a bio-baby compared to the flourishing industries based on the micro-chip. But as it grows up over the next decade and is harnessed alongside other technologies (micro-bugs alongside micro-chips), it will transform the food and drugs industry.

Not least among conceivable changes startling enough to make blood pressures rise (but involving new ways of keeping them down) is the possibility of extending the normal human life span to ninety or one hundred years. Research is under way to develop products that will delay ageing. If successful, this could produce a grey revolution of stunning implications for work and retirement. Who will want to retire at sixty, after forty years' work, if they have another forty years of life ahead of them? But how can they be given jobs if robots replace people?

No one can be sure exactly what new industries will flourish in the next century as a result of new technologies. What is clear is that these technologies are combining to reveal both undreamed of opportunities and the possibility of an unprecedented destruction of jobs. What people want to know is whether the jobs created by these opportunities will exceed the number destroyed. Will society be left with more or less jobs as a result of it all? And what does this mean for unemployment? Will we ever get back to the full employment of the 1950s and 1960s?

THE RETURN OF WORK

Three possibilities have been suggested. They can be labelled the return of work, the collapse of work and the change of work views. Return of work supporters say that new technologies will eventually create enough jobs to reduce unemployment substantially. Many of these jobs will be in activities which are difficult to envisage now, but they will be similar to today's work in that most people will be employed in one occupation for thirty-five to forty hours a week.

Waves of jobs

Many people are in a hurry to dismiss this view. They are surprised that anyone can take it seriously. It is obvious, they think, that new technologies will prevent rather than provide a return to full employment as we knew it. However, many of our leading politicians believe in the return of work. Mrs Thatcher said in 1984 that Britain was experiencing a third industrial revolution. The point had been reached where new technologies were opening up possibilities for new jobs, but some old industries were still shedding labour. 'The first stage of the new technology tends to put people out of work. The second stage tends to create all kinds of jobs that didn't exist previously. We are in the interim now. I hope that this year will be the stage where...we will have the levelling off and then be able to go into a regenerative process...the revival is starting and we want it to gather pace.'

A fairly sophisticated argument has been wheeled out to support the return of work view. It dates – ironically for Mrs Thatcher – from the Russian economist, Nikolai Kondratiev, who was Director of Applied Economic Research in Moscow before being banished to Siberia in 1930. An updated version of Kondratiev's theory goes something like this: If you look at the history of the industrialized West over the last 200 years, you can spot 'long waves' of business activity. (These are not to be confused with Alvin Toffler's three waves, which are very different.)

The troughs between the waves are periods of high unemployment. They are also times when clusters of major technical break-throughs occur. These break-throughs centred on cotton, iron and agriculture in the mid-eighteenth century; on rail, steam and steel in the 1820s; electricity and chemicals in the 1880s; aerospace, electronics and further developments in chemicals in the 1930s and 1940s; and information technologies, energy and biotech materials in the 1970s and 1980s.

Jobs are spawned as new industries climb on the back of these developments. The number of jobs peak at the crest of the wave, but turn down as the industries which created the jobs pass the phase of rapid growth. Unemployment then rises and a new trough is reached, till the process of innovation and job creation takes the economy to the crest of a new wave. On this view, major inventions in the middle of this century generated a multitude of jobs in the 1950s, 1960s and early 1970s. The flow of jobs then slowed as saturation of the market reduced the scope for expanding output and scores of companies got in on the act. The increase in competition encouraged factory automation which slashed the number of workers hired.

So, for example, following technical developments in the 1930s and 1940s, a mass of jobs flowed from the mushrooming TV industry after the war. The total number of people employed in the production of TV sets began to tail off, however, as each house came to have one and as production techniques were refined to reduce the amount of labour required. With the same happening in a number of industries, a trough has now been reached between the jobs created by earlier innovations and the work which will be thrown up by a cluster of new technologies.

The main feature of these technologies is their phenomenal potential to create wealth. The amount produced by each person could rise dramatically. But this will not reduce jobs, say the return of work advocates. Remember, they say, that the technologies which kill jobs are not the same as the technologies which give birth to jobs. People displaced from farms during the industrial revolution never got work on the farms again. What advances in farm technology did was to create huge food surpluses which allowed the labour force to move into the cities and the factories. More recently, improvements in manufacturing technology (the introduction of numerically-controlled machines, for instance, and greater automation generally) have produced the wealth to pay for an expansion of banking, entertainment, health, education and other 'services', while reducing the size of factory workforces. From 1961 to 1981 over 2 million jobs in Britain shifted from manufacturing to services.

New technologies will continue this trend. As each person produces more he or she will be paid more, and therefore will be able to buy more. People will be employed in producing all sorts of new goods and services to satisfy this extra demand. There will be a continuing massive expansion of the service sector in particular. As a taste of things to come, a new breed of professional recreationists is emerging in the United States to design creative leisure pursuits. A plethora of new occupations, like this, can be expected to pop up in the least expected places, just as jobs have always been produced in the past.

That we cannot predict precisely what what these new jobs will be should come as no surprise. After all, when the aeroplane was invented, who could have guessed at the range of jobs that would be propelled into existence as a result? Apart from jobs in producing, maintaining and flying the aircraft, millions of jobs have been created in tourism which extends from the holiday trade to the conference business, and which in its present form is critically dependent on air travel.

Just as it is hard to envisage modern society without the plane, so, some say, the time will come when it will be difficult to imagine our world without the millions of jobs produced by today's new technologies. Our children will take jobs lasting thirty-five to forty hours a week as much for granted as we do. Or will they?

Waving goodbye

The sceptics are not convinced, not least because they are unsure that the return-to-workers have taken full account of the size of the task ahead. Not only must jobs be provided for those who currently have none; they must also be found for the growing number of people who are likely to be seeking work. One problem (which we saw in chapter two) is that if many new jobs become available, some of those who gave up looking for employment can be expected to resume the search.

In the economy of the future, an expansion of work opportunities will draw more people into the job queue. Among them are likely to be those who would otherwise have considered themselves to be retired, thereby reversing the trend toward early retirement. Married women would probably feature in particularly large numbers. For there is no reason to suppose that the tendency, which tailed off with the recession, for more wives to want jobs would not continue again if work became available.

Should the number of wives wanting work reach Scandinavian proportions, an extra 2.75 million people in Britain could be looking for jobs by the turn of the century. A more cautious estimate, assuming jobs were available, would put the figure at 1.25 million. Clearly there is plenty of room for error! But the point stands out: to reduce unemployment to below 1 million by the year 2000, jobs will have to be provided not only for the 2 to 3 million who are signed on now, but also (on the higher figure) for the same number again who will be joining the national job hunt. It is a daunting task.

It presents a formidable challenge to those who believe in long waves. Plainly a ripple of new jobs will not be enough. More like a tidal wave is required. Yet the promise of jobs in the future is an act of faith. Even though jobs have been created in the past, no one can be sure the same will happen again. Repetition is less certain if – as is the case with supposed long waves – there are only a handful of previous experiences to go on (at the most, four). It becomes less certain still if many experts dispute that jobs were created through a wave-like process in the first place.

Historians are generally sceptical, to say the least, about long waves. They doubt that innovation, job-creation and unemployment fit the neat wave-like pattern Kondratiev's followers would like. As one historian has remarked, plenty of examples 'show that any very rigid and stereotyped version of the course of the international economy must be qualified out of recognition.' Waves – as a law of history – can be waved goodbye.

The key point is that many of the new technologies are not at all like the old. Previous inventions increased physical power and found new applications for it – the steamship replaced sail, the car the horse, and so on. But their operation was dependent on the human brain. Sewing machines, typewriters, manually operated telephones and motor cars were all designed to have one operator for each machine, which created hosts of jobs. By contrast, micro-based technologies are intended to take over certain functions of the brain and to reduce, if not eliminate, human intervention. They provide brain power as well as increasing brawn power.

Clive Sinclair, of micro-computer fame, has written about his vision of the future in which there will be a robot slave for everyone. The Japanese and Americans are learning to make robots which can see and feel. Robotic brains are evolving at a fantastic rate. 'Tomorrow we may take our ailments to a machine as readily as to a man,' says Sinclair. 'In time that machine will be in the house, removing the need to journey to the doctor and providing a far more regular monitoring of the state of health than it is now economic to provide. The computer as surrogate teacher may bring even greater benefits... The advantage of a tutor for each child is clear, and if that tutor is endlessly patient and super-humanly well-informed, we may expect a wonderful improvement in the standard of education.'

If it becomes possible to automate these and other 'service' tasks – and many, in banking for instance, are already being taken over by machines – where will all the jobs of the future come from? If the 'service' sector, which is the main hope of future jobs, can itself be robotized – robot barmen are serving up to thirty mixes in California – must we not expect that the micro will leave us with a micro labour force? Do not the foundations of the return of work view collapse?

As the technological juggernaut rumbles on relentlessly, we must look forward to changes as fundamental as those produced by the industrial revolution 200 years ago. And just as the car is a poor guide to the environmental impact of the juggernaut, so the industrial system of the past will provide few signposts to high-tech patterns of work in the future. It is time the political establishment proclaimed loudly that work as we have known it, on the scale we have known it, will never return. We could then debate more widely what should take its place.

THE COLLAPSE OF WORK

The opposite view, the 'collapse of work' argument, has achieved notoriety largely through the books jointly written by trade union officials Clive Jenkins and Barry Sherman. They expect new techologies to chip away at one job after another with robotic monotony, producing a relentless climb in unemployment. The landmarks of their picture are the speed of change, the size of the job losses and the small scope for new jobs to replace the old.

With robots already making robots and computers writing computer programmes, very few jobs produced by the micro-chip can avoid being replaced by the micro-chip, they say. Where new technologies do create jobs, it will only be a matter of time before the bulk of these jobs are gobbled up by another machine. Ahead lies the 'leisure shock' – a future in which people do not know what to do. Only by educating for leisure now can the shock of the new technologies be absorbed.

Exaggerates the speed of change

This look at the future almost certainly exaggerates the pace at which new technologies will be introduced. A company, 'Info-Tech' may have the most superb office automation package for sale, involving electronic filing, sophisticated teleconferencing facilities, and equipment for the paperless transfer of information which would make the waste-paper bin as delightfully obsolete as inkwells are today. But orders will come slowly if there are not enough technicians to install the equipment, if software specialists cannot be found to programme computers and if management does not know how to make best use of the facilities. All the evidence suggests that skill shortages are delaying the introduction of new technologies, often by long periods. In some skills, the shortage is chronic.

Nor will Info-Tech sales be helped by some of the technical obstacles that exist. The 'haves' of office automation cannot easily communicate with the 'have nots'. Why should a potential customer hurry to install Info-Tech's expensive equipment if it will improve communication with only one in ten of its clients? Or if head office will be unable to communicate electronically with its branches because they lack the necessary equipment and cannot afford to buy it? Or if it will face problems in linking some of its existing computers with the new system because they are incompatible? Or if installing the new equipment will involve writing off the older word-processors and the like on which sizeable sums were spent only recently? Such obstacles do not halt progress: they just mean that the immediate prospect of a paperless office on every floor may be little more than a paper tiger.

Exaggerates the number of jobs lost

The collapse of work view may also exaggerate the number of employees who will have their work axed. Economic forecasting even for one year ahead, when the certainties are relatively great, is notoriously difficult. So predictions involving huge unknowns over a much longer period should be treated with the thorough scepticism they deserve. Mark Twain's comment is rather apt: 'There is something fascinating about science – one gets such wholesale return of conjecture out of such a trifling investment of fact.'

The worst nightmares of 'automatic' unemployment assume that new equipment will be used with maximum efficiency, displacing the maximum number of people, but experience shows that this is rarely the case. Even Info-Tech, which makes the equipment, might find that its employees do not take full advantage of it. Certain computer facilities may be left unused because top staff are not aware of their potential.

In addition, the popular idea of far fewer secretaries working in tomorrow's office because so many of their tasks have been taken over by machines may be false. In Info-Tech's futuristic offices (installed partly to impress the customers), secretaries may continue to be very much in evidence. As one of today's bosses remarked, 'I don't want a machine. I want my secretary so that she can look after the clients – bring the coffee, show them around, impress them with friendliness – and be generally available to me.' It has been said that we live in a polygamous society. A boss may have one wife at home and another at work. The last thing he will want is for his work wife to be displaced by technology (though whether secretaries will wish to continue their wifely role is another matter). Social pressures will resist the automation of some jobs.

It may be that technology will change the nature of the job rather than destroy it. At Info-Tech, typing, filing and other routine tasks may be delegated to machines, enabling secretaries to become more like managerial assistants with a greater share in decision-making. June, who started life as a copy-typist, may be sent on a company course to learn how to interpret statistics. Clive Sinclair's dream of mechanical teaching and robotized doctors may ignore how these jobs will change too. The emphasis of the GP's work may shift from diagnosing illness to helping patients cope with the pressures of life, so that they will be less prone to stress-related ailments. With the growing number of marriage breakdowns, teachers may be asked increasingly to give children the emotional support lacking at home.

Lack of efficiency, social resistance and changes in the nature of the job may well act as a brake on the number of jobs lost through new technologies. Interestingly enough, a survey of the effects of micro-electronics on manufacturing confirms that the great job-loss scare may be exaggerated. Micro-electronics caused a net drop of 34,000 jobs between 1981 and 1983 – less than one in twenty of the total fall in manufacturing jobs over that period. This should make us very cautious about the view that new technologies will lead to a rapid decline in jobs.

Exaggerates the absence of new work

It has often been noticed that those in the midst of a social revolution are the last to know it is going on. Perhaps if our eyes were open, we would see more clearly the signs of a profound consumer revolution, typified by this observation: whereas twenty years ago tourists would drive around Scotland in British-built Morris Minors to buy made-in-Japan souvenirs, now they are more likely to be driving a Japanese Mitsubishi and to be on the lookout for genuine Highland crafts. If Britain's mushrooming cottage industries were gathered together, they would represent a craft city of no mean size.

This change in consumer taste suggests that many new jobs will replace those destroyed by technology. If machines appear to push us into the wings, the likely human response will be to seek new ways of taking centre stage. To receive a letter that begins, 'Dear 48763, we have a personal interest in you...' will no longer be a joke, but a reminder of the highly threatening, impersonal world in which we find ourselves. The search could be on to find how human touches can be brought into an increasingly mechanized society. We will look for ways to personalize an impersonal world – to express our worth and retain our identity.

This should cause no surprise, for despite the initial fascination with gadgetry, after a while interest usually focuses less on what the machine can do than on what people can do with the machine. A photograph is normally admired not chiefly because of the type of camera and lens involved, but because of the skill and imagination employed in taking it. People are willing to pay for the artistry behind a photograph. It is the human angle in life which appeals, and work is more and more likely to reflect this. So we can almost certainly expect a continued 'back to the crafts' reaction in the search for products reflecting individual character. Furniture, for example, with all the marks of a craftsman's personality, may become steadily more sought after than that which is mass-produced.

Alongside the growing demand for personalized products is likely to be a greater demand for personal services. Despite the current expansion of self-catering holidays, self-service restaurants and self-service shopping for those on middle and lower incomes, those who can afford it still prefer the cost of being waited upon. The demand for this service can be expected to increase as high technology, soaring still higher, creates the wealth for more people to pay for it. Top quality service involves treating the customer with respect, as an individual, and this is precisely what people will want when machines seem to dehumanize their lives. So watch out for an expansion of all sorts of luxury entertainment in which the quality of personal service is a key ingredient. People-to-people work could be one of tomorrow's major job generators.

The growing popularity of do-it-yourself reflects a similar quest for the personal, quite apart from the need to stretch one's income. In this case, the individual is not looking to buy someone else's personalized product or service. Instead, by improving the home, repairing the car and exchanging skills, he or she finds an outlet for his or her own abilities. The 'Network', sponsored by the Merseyside Council for Voluntary Service, is one example of a number of organizations which are trying to help people with requests for time, skills or goods to contact others able to meet their needs. No money is exchanged. One skill is swapped for another. Time is exchanged for time (for example, baby-minding for granny-minding); goods are traded for goods. In this way, DIY is going commercial in a cashless way. It illustrates how skills fashioned in the home are increasingly being shared with others to earn (in cash or kind) a bit on the side.

Many foresee continued growth of this 'side-work', which we can think of as hobbies or voluntary-type activities done for other people on a casual basis. Some of it will be unpaid, consisting of tasks done within the home or in the community: weeding the church garden, helping with meals-on-wheels, looking after an elderly relative next door. Some of it will be paid, perhaps in kind rather than in cash, as with skill-swapping, or in payments which form part of the 'black economy' because they are never declared to the taxman. Whatever its precise form, there are plenty of opportunities – carpentry, painting, toy-making, car maintenance, pottery, vegetable growing, tree-pruning, home-brewing, dressmaking, interior decorating, upholstery, typing, reading scripts, translating, tutoring, picture-painting, computer programming, and so on. The list is almost endless, and is likely to grow as the demand for personalized goods and services comes together with the desire to work in a more 'human' way to supply them.

New technologies may themselves increase the opportunities for side-work. Videos, for example, have created their own market in a short space of time in the high street. And they are likely to create another market in home movies, in which the skills of certain individuals are recognized and rewarded. 'You can use my computer game if I can borrow your video.' As more such requests are made, what started as a form of leisure may become part-time work in which the activity is increasingly pursued to get something else. For a gifted person, the part-time work may become full-time. The booming market in home-programmed computer games, swapped or sold among young people, illustrates the same point.

Though the pay may be less, side-work has many advantages over part or full-time 'job-work'. The individual has greater control over what he or she is doing. She can do more or less what she wants, when she wants. He can decorate for a few hours and then take the children to the park. Her time is not governed by the schedule of a supervisor. There can be more variety – working in the garden one minute, mending a chair the next and helping to decorate a neighbour's house after that. There is greater scope for initiative, too, for the individual is not hemmed in by the rules of an employer. Above all, he brings more of himself to the task. His work is not dominated by some machine whose regular movements force a day-long mechanical response from the person using it. Rather, his work expresses his own character more fully. It provides welcome relief for the individual who has switched off from the push-button society.

A survey in 1982 found 750,000 more people working in Britain than expected. They were clearly service activities, but did not fit any of the statistical categories within services (hotels and catering, education, business services, and so on). So the statisticians classified them in the 'miscellaneous' category within services, and within 'miscellaneous' they assigned them to a sub-section entitled 'miscellaneous'! No one knows quite what these jobs are (except, of course, those doing them), but they are almost certainly part-time, and many are likely to come close to our description of side-work. They probably contain some of the growth occupations of the future.

Side-work, often as a supplement to job-work, can be expected to go on expanding, and its status to improve. It is officially discouraged at present because supplementary benefit is reduced if the unemployed earn more than £4 a week (in cash or kind) and declare it. In some cases these earnings are not declared, payments for small jobs becoming part of the norm. If side-work grows in importance, official attitudes will have to change.

Independence, freedom and self-sufficiency are already virtues in our society. Demonstrating these virtues by providing for your own needs – brewing your own beer, growing your own vegetables and producing your own entertainment – instead of relying on someone else, may come to be seen as the first step to success. The next step may be to turn self-sufficiency into a business in which you can display further signs of success: the freedom to work from home, the ability to get your own business and the capacity to be your own boss. Whereas it was a sign of success to pay other people to do or make all you need, perhaps success will increasingly be measured by one's independence. Fashions do change!

THE CHANGE OF WORK

Instead of the collapse of work view (which exaggerates the speed of change, the number of jobs lost and the shortage of new ones) changes in the nature of work are likely. Changes can be expected on four fronts.

The first will be **a change in the nature of jobs**. In tomorrow's world, the skills required in job-work will be different, and jobs will be concentrated more and more in the service sector and in information (not least education and entertainment). In 1983, services and information accounted for 68 per cent of all jobs in the United States, and 63 per cent in the United Kingdom. This bias away from manufacturing is likely to become even more marked, partly through the accelerating pace of automation made possible by new technologies, and partly as companies shift traditional industry to the Third World.

In some cases, as with the birth of the Middle East petro-chemical industry, the aim of the move south will be to get closer to raw materials and to save on transport costs. In others, companies will take advantage of poor countries' lower wages and longer working hours to cut labour costs. With firms using similar production techniques around the world, savings in these areas may give a vital competitive edge. It all adds up to what is known (in a ghastly phrase) as the process of deindustrialization. Many who hold to the 'return of work' theory would go along with this. The 'change of work' view differs by saying that there will not be enough new service jobs to offset fully the decline in manufac-turing work.

So, not only will the nature of jobs alter, but there will also be **a change in the number of jobs**. New technologies will continue to invade the services, as is already happening in banking and insurance, and this will reduce jobs available. True, the number of people-to-people jobs in the services is likely to grow (in education, for example). But these and other new jobs are unlikely to provide work for all those displaced from manufacturing. So an overall decline in jobs is probable, though it will not be as sharp as the 'collapse of work' view predicts.

Third, there will be **a change in the length of jobs**. On present trends, a growing number of new jobs will be part-time. In 1983 there were 1.3 million more part-time jobs in Britain than there had been a decade earlier. Nearly all were in the service sector, and a number were prime jobs: on check-out desks, reception tills, office accountancy machines, and so on. A large majority were filled by women. By contrast, 2.5 million full-time male jobs had disappeared since the mid-1960s. A serious mismatch had devel-oped between men losing their jobs and women taking the new part-time ones. If the trend towards part-time work continues – one estimate reckons that a quarter of Britain's workforce will be in part-time jobs by the end of the century – men may have to become more flexible in their choice of employment. Already in the United States men are more willing than their British counterparts to work in the service industries, and to work part-time if necessary. If this is the direction in which we have to move, can ways be found to make the change less painful for those involved?

Finally, for the reasons already described, the expansion of side-work will lead to **a change in the importance of jobs**. Side-work will be less formal, less regular and less geared towards cash payments than part-time job-work. It will find its place somewhere between hobbies and part-time work in prime jobs – rather like the odd jobs now done in the black economy. More side-work is likely despite official discouragement. As side-work increases, full and part-time work in prime jobs will become less important. Jobs will still have a central role, but alongside them will grow a number of alternatives. One of the great unknowns, however, is how full-time jobs, part-time jobs and side-work will be distributed. Who will do what?

Change for the better

Let us take the case of Stuart, early in the next century. He is a thirty-year old technician in a company that is striding ahead in pursuit of avant-garde technologies. The office is highly automated, but there is a quiet relaxation about the place. Plenty of people are around, a number of them clients. Some are waiting for their appointments, but none are sitting on their own. The low buzz of conversation includes the chat between the waiting clients and the personal assistants assigned to them, as they drink what seems to be endless cups of coffee.

Few repetitive jobs can be seen in the office or in the factory below. As elsewhere on the industrial estate, most traditional employees such as sprayers and welders, machine tool operators, packers and bottlers, copy typists, filing clerks and others in comparable work found they were replaced by the micro-chip at some stage over the past twenty-five years. Often their jobs just disappeared.

Sometimes their occupations were completely transformed. Audio and copy typists with a flair for layout and presentation found their skills no longer required because word-processors could do the job in a fraction of the time. They are the ones to be seen minding the machines. The lucky people are the personal assistants. They used to be secretaries, but technology has relieved them of the more repetitive and tedious aspects of filing and typing. They now have time to help managers analyze the volume of information produced by the knowledge revolution. The assistant chatting to the client by the window will play an important part in the meeting that is about to begin.

Quite a few of those in the office on this particular morning are in jobs created by technical change. There is a high-tech consultant, come to show how the latest technology can be used to the best advantage. The software specialists are advising on the cataloguing of computer programmes (the catalogue has got into an awful mess). Hardware repair and maintenance staff are having a meeting. And then there are those employed in creative design, research and development and a host of tasks which filter, analyze and interpret information. These jobs have become surprisingly numerous because new technologies have widened their scope. At the far end of the floor are stairs to the Personnel Department. There, unknown to the rest of the staff, a decision is being taken to hire a consultant to advise on improving relationships among full-time staff and network contractors.

Network contracting is uppermost in Stuart's mind this morning. Most of his friends are doing it. Why shouldn't he? But it is not an easy decision. Over the years, the normal working week has shrunk to the equivalent of thirty hours. Time has been carved up so that Stuart can either work three forty-hour weeks with every fourth week off (plus extra weeks as holidays), or he can work for three four-day weeks followed by a three-day week. Stuart has chosen the latter. He likes the regular mix of days on and off.

The rising salary from Stuart's job-work – not to mention the income of his wife, Claire – has enabled his family to spend more on sports and other kinds of recreation. They often go to Paris for a weekend. On his days off, Stuart also does side-work. He repairs his friends' home gadgets and they decorate his house in return. He also grows highly-valued shrubs on his allotment. Stuart especially enjoys the flexibility of his side-work. He can break off from a repair job to drive his son to the ice-rink, or help his daughter write a new computer game. There is plenty of space for people. And he is his own boss. At the same time, he can be sure of a regular and decent income from his job as a technician.

But Stuart is frightened that he will get stuck in a rut. At the age of thirty he has got everything he wants – well, almost. Stuart is no mean swimmer, and he has been offered a part-time job as an instructor. He would love to accept, but to do so would mean that he would have less time to spend with his family or on his existing side-work, both of which he enjoys. The answer would be to do what his friends have done, which is to network. Stuart would become self-employed and would contract to work for his present company for the equivalent of twenty hours a week. He would have to take a drop in salary, of course, but this would largely be offset by his instructor's pay.

The snag is that his job-work would be less secure as a contractor. In times of recession, when the company has to cut back, contractors are always the first to suffer. Also, because

Stuart lives an age of rapid technological change, it is likely that he will need retraining at some stage. Again, the company gives priority to its full-time staff. Is he prepared to pay for his own retraining? Stuart wonders.

On the other hand, even if he does stay full-time, his job will never be 100 per cent secure. Other full-timers have been made redundant. But as a contractor, he might be able to pick up some jobs with other firms, reducing the number of hours he was contracted to his present employer. This would not only provide welcome variety; it might also increase his job security since he would not be totally dependent on one firm. Stuart can see arguments for and against. It is not an easy choice, he thinks to himself.

But at least he has a choice. In this picture of how work could change, not only will job-work differ from today in the skills required, in the number of hours involved and in the larger numbers self-employed, but people will have far more options than at present. It will be possible to combine all sorts of work in a variety of ways. Some people would work the equivalent of thirty hours a week in job-work (possibly in more than one job), while others, out of choice, would work less, perhaps only ten hours. All the combinations will involve fewer hours in high paid job-work than at present, give more opportunities for lower paid side-work and encourage a richer diversity of leisure pursuits. Unemployment would be relatively low, and would consist mainly of those who had left one job and were waiting to start another.

Change for the worse

The flip side of this story sees Stuart as one of a sizeable elite in job-work. The bulk of this elite work thirty-two to thirty-five hours a week. Because relatively few of them work part-time, it has been impossible to share the well-paid and highly desirable job-work around the population as a whole. Many people only have side-work or no work at all. Stuart, though, is doing very nicely in his job. On the basis of a steadily rising income, he has a mortgage on a pleasant suburban home where he lives with his family. But one day he hears that his job is to be replaced by a machine: he is to be made redundant.

At first Stuart thinks that with his skills it will be easy to get another job. But almost as big a shock as losing his job is the discovery that so many technicians like him are unemployed, too. He had no idea his skills had become so outdated. Slowly, the possibility that he will not find another job begins to dawn. Stuart manages to earn a little – over and above his benefit – by doing odd jobs for others. But this scarcely compensates for the huge fall in his income. The Building Society allowes him to postpone his mortgage payments for a while, but not indefinitely. Only limited help is available from government.

Like many others in his position, Stuart is forced to sell up. But his wife, Claire, cannot face the move which will signal to her friends that she has married a failure. She is fed up as it is with Stuart mooching around the house all day. The row last night was the last straw. She walks out, taking the children with her. Stuart is left to reflect on the contrast between his well-paid, high-tech life, and life on the dole supplemented by odd bits of side-work. Side-work was all right on the side, but there is not enough of it and the pay is too low to compensate for the lack of job-work.

Stuart has seen both sides of a society divided even more sharply than today, between those with decent jobs and those without. Many fear that changes in work brought about by new technologies will usher in that division on a permanent basis. There will be a chasm between those with the deluxe job-work, and those with second class side-work (if they work at all). One of the key issues today is whether steps can be taken to prevent that split. Can different forms of work be combined to produce a better future rather than a worse one?

CONCLUSION

What we think about the return of work, collapse of work and change of work views has huge implications for today. It will affect what we teach people at school, for example. If we believe that eventually there will be a return to full employment like we had in the 1950s and 1960s (as some still seem to believe), we shall be less likely to call for radical changes in the curriculum. On the other hand, if we expect work to collapse, we shall want to train young people to resist the impending 'leisure shock'.

If, however, we go for the more likely view that the nature of work will change, we would be wise to prepare people for changes in the nature of jobs, number of jobs, length of jobs and importance of jobs. Not least we shall need to encourage people to be flexible in their attitudes to work – to abandon the idea of a life-long career, to be willing to switch jobs, to train for new jobs and to develop new forms of side-work.

More generally, what we need is a strategy that harnesses the wealth-creating power of new technologies but also takes account

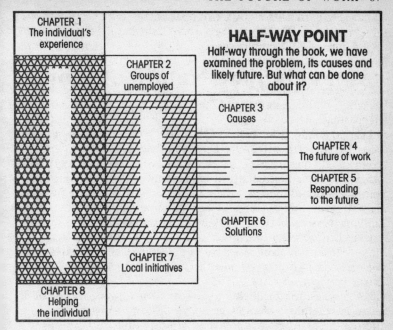

HALF-WAY POINT
Half-way through the book, we have examined the problem, its causes and likely future. But what can be done about it?

CHAPTER 1
The individual's experience

CHAPTER 2
Groups of unemployed

CHAPTER 3
Causes

CHAPTER 4
The future of work

CHAPTER 5
Responding to the future

CHAPTER 6
Solutions

CHAPTER 7
Local initiatives

CHAPTER 8
Helping the individual

of their impact on jobs. We need to tackle today's unemployment in a way that promotes the change-for-the-better scenario's attractive mix of different types of work, rather than the change-for-the-worse division between those with plum jobs and those without.

We have seen how it feels to be out of work, how the needs of the unemployed vary, what some of the explanations for unemployment are and what the future of work could be like. The task now is to find principles to guide our thinking about work, and to develop an action-plan based on those principles.

CHAPTER 5

Changing the Nature of Work

THE MEANING OF WORK
For those with a job

It is an odd fact that people who believe work is a good thing often find their particular job unpleasant or dull. Filling in their football coupons launches them on a fantasy flight away from the daily routine. For there is not much glamour in shovelling stinking toxic waste, or working near the sweltering heat of a furnace, or washing up endless dishes in a kitchen, or sitting at a supermarket checkout all day. People take these jobs because they have to. They are chained to the workbench by the rewards of work.

Take Gill, for example. She works on a word-processor in London. Each day she makes the tiring commuter journey from the depths of Kent to a job that is pretty dull. Little thought is required from her at work. All that is expected is that she complete her routine tasks day after day. Yet the possibility of losing her job would fill Gill with horror. The job itself may not be exciting, but it has paid enough for an active social life, as well as a holiday in Greece. It has brought her the company of others at work. She can tell them all sorts of things about her boyfriend which she could never discuss at home.

And it has given her a degree of self-confidence. The income has made her an independent person. She is free to do live away from home. She feels good having a measure of control over her life. It feels good, too, to be doing something worthwhile. Although when she gets her pay cheque her thoughts are on how to spend it, deep down there is a sense of being valued. She is worth being paid. For Gill, work brings cash, company and confidence.

For those without

Given the occult-like grip of work on the individual, it is only to be expected that those who lose it should experience considerable distress. 'We want to find our faith in unemployment,' exclaimed John, who had been out of work for two years. His cry was on behalf of a multitude of dazed and despondent jobless people, who seek meaning in lives which float aimlessly from day to day, slowly turning around an invisible point. They want to recreate the sense of purpose that work gave them. But in what can they put their faith? They can hardly believe in themselves.

Imagine Terry. He has felt a failure all his life. He was no good at school (though he scraped a couple of CSEs) and was not exactly a high flier on one of the youth training schemes (but he did stay the course). Since then he has tried to get work, but each time his application has been rejected. And that is precisely how he feels – a reject. Faith for Terry is not to be found in himself.

Nor is it to be found in friends. Terry has been unemployed now for eighteen months. When he came off the youth training scheme, life was not so bad. Quite a few of his mates were out of work, too. They walked the streets, 'did a few places' and passed away the time. It was scarcely the high life, but at least he had company. Gradually, they drifted apart, however. With little to do, there was not much to keep them together. Terry still ambles along the streets each evening. Now, though, he is in the company not of friends but of strangers. His has become an isolated existence. There is not much comfort in friends.

Of course, Terry thinks, it would be all right if only he had the money. At least he could afford a drink and buy those little luxuries that make life bearable. Yet by the time he has paid food and board to his parents (absentee landlords he calls them, because they are out all day and hardly speak to him in the evening), not much of his benefit is left. Bored for so long, he finds himself smoking more than he did and spending what little is left on chocolate – to fill in time. He used to try to save enough for a pint at weekends, but he never managed it. There's no point in trying any more. Clearly, so long as he remains out of work, money cannot be a source of meaning for Terry.

Each unemployed person has a different story, but for many the basic theme is the same. They lack the cash, company and confidence that paid work can bring, and without these life has little purpose. Too often, as we saw in chapter one, an axed job leaves an emotional stump.

WORK IS NOT THE BASIS OF WORTH

Most people perhaps feel that their worth is in some way bound up with their job. When we are introduced to somebody, one of the first things we want to know is what he or she does. The more important the job, we are inclined to think, the more important the person. Self-esteem is so tied up with work that often a person made redundant will go on seeing himself in terms of his previous occupation. A fitter in the shipyards may still think of himself as a fitter two years after losing his job. Gill and Terry certainly see work as a source of personal worth. Gill feels good partly because having a job means that she is valued enough to be paid monthly. Terry's life fell apart because not having one made him feel a failure and left him with nothing to do. But need it have done? Was he right to value himself in terms of whether he had paid work? Or can self-esteem come from a different source?

The Protestant work ethic

To answer these questions, we need to examine the Protestant work ethic, which has given the West many of its ideals about work. Broadly speaking, the Protestant work ethic, which emerged during the sixteenth and seventeenth centuries, encouraged the idea that work was a moral duty. God created the human race, the theologians said, to serve God by means of work. Through work man and woman were to look after creation and meet the needs of other people. So, when Gill goes to work she is doing what God intended. If she were not working, she would have every reason to feel guilty because she would not be serving God in the way that he wants.

Some theologians took this idea a stage further. They said that if Christians were successful in work, this was evidence that God had accepted them – that they were among 'the elect' who would go to heaven rather than hell. A booming business was a blessing from God, showing his approval of your life. So the idea grew up that success in work – profitable business ventures, plenty of customers or whatever – was a sign of being valued by God. It took only a small but decisive step for later generations to assume that work was not merely a sign that one was valued, but the source itself of that value. You were a worthwhile person because you worked. Today, the status and income of a job is commonly thought to reflect the worth of the person holding it.

It is important to stress that the Protestant work ethic did not say that work itself was the source of worth. That is a more modern belief. At most it said that success in work could be a sign that one was saved, that one had joined the elect. Even though this view is unfashionable now, other aspects of the Protestant work ethic have remained popular. Not least is the still widespread idea that work is a moral duty.

This is one reason why Terry's parents will hardly speak to him. They think he *ought* to be working. 'He ought to have a job,' his father keeps muttering. However angry Terry feels with his parents, he cannot escape the fact that deep inside he agrees with them. He feels he should have a job not simply for the money, but because somehow he is doing wrong by not working. Secretly, behind the brave face, there is a nagging sense of guilt.

This guilt compounds his feelings of failure. It is bad enough for Terry to be rejected by one employer after another and to live in a society that believes that no job makes you a nobody. All this is sufficiently burdensome without the weight of guilt being added as well, without the Protestant work ethic making life still hotter for the unemployed. But ironically, if we bypass the Protestant work ethic and go back to the ideas of the Bible itself, we can discover the basis for a new, liberating definition of work.

A different angle on work

Many Christians today believe that the Protestant work ethic, as it has come to be understood, is a fundamental misinterpretation of what the Bible says about work and its relation to personal value. It certainly does not do justice to the strong biblical idea that work is *not* the basis of human worth. In the Bible's account of creation, man and woman were made great because they were given many of the characteristics of God himself (they were created in the 'image of God'). Having been made God-like in many ways, man and woman were then given the command to work. In other words, human greatness came before people started to work, not afterwards. This is a major reversal of the popular view that human status comes not before work but through it. Terry and Gill saw work as the means to self-worth, as a way to become valuable people. The Bible, on the other hand, says that they are valuable before they have worked.

How valuable they are is spelt out in the rest of the Bible. At the beginning of the Old Testament, man and woman turn their backs on God, which leads to a breakdown in their relationship with him. It is commonplace in our society for relationships to break down. They certainly had in Terry's family. His parents scarcely spoke to him. His father called him a 'no hoper'. Terry's reaction was to seethe with rage. The minute he got a job, he would say to himself (in his less despairing moments), he would leave home, and if ever his parents were in any difficulty, don't let them come to him for help!

God's response to the rupture in man and woman's friendship with him was in marked contrast. His love for the people he had made not only survived their rejection of him, but overcame it. The New Testament talks about God sending his Son to die so that his friendship with people could be restored. That is how important Terry and Gill are to him. Their worth lies not in a particular job, but in the fact that God so values them that he cannot bear – even if it cost Jesus his life – to be separated from them. Their humanity, not their work, gives their lives meaning.

Seeing work in this context can bring great relief to the unemployed. There is a voice inside Terry which tells him that he is a failure, that he is no good, that no one wants him. Jesus Christ died to silence that voice. It is as if two people were walking in the countryside. There is a rock in the path. To one of the hikers the rock is of no value. He moves to push it away. His friend, who is a sculptor, stops him. 'Don't push it away,' he says. 'It may seem no use to you, but I can see in it a beautiful sculpture. Let me take it home and bring out the beauty that lies within it.' So the sculptor takes the rock, chisels away and turns it into an exquisite masterpiece.

God says something similar to Terry and all the unemployed who are in despair. 'Don't listen to the voice of failure. It's not telling you the truth. It's not telling you what I see in you. In you there is an exquisite masterpiece. Allow me to chisel away, to bring out the beauty inside you and to make you into the person I want you to be. I died so that I could do this. Won't you let me have a go?' The Bible says that if the jobless will listen to God their lives will be transformed. Feelings of failure will give way to the knowledge of acceptance. To borrow a phrase, Christ died that the unemployed might laugh again.

From work ethic to life ethic

This view of worth and work could be a great encouragement to Terry. It would help to counter his sense of failure and rejection. Other people may have turned him down when he applied for jobs, but the God who is more important than anyone has accepted him and wants to turn him into a masterpiece. 'That's a great thought!' Terry might say to himself. 'It's as if the site foreman thinks I'm no good, but here comes the Managing Director, and what does he say? "Leave it to me. This lad is just the person I want in my office. You think he's no good, but I know better than that. I know all about him. He's just the person to help me run the company." Hey,' Terry might laugh, 'I wonde what the foreman would think about that!'

The idea that worth precedes work is so important that it should be given some form of community expression. It should be reflected, for example, in social security arrangements to show that it is a truth in which society as a whole believes. The ideal might be to do this through what is sometimes described as the social wage.

In its simplest form the social wage would replace the present complex social security benefits. Government would pay a straight cash sum to every individual whatever her or his age, marital status or abilities, and whether they were working or not. Both Terry and Gill, irrespective of whether they had a job, would receive a state payment large enough to guarantee them a reasonable standard of living. (It would have to be considerably more than the existing supplementary benefit.)

Though the same amount would be paid to everyone whether they worked or not, the connection between work and income would not be completely broken. Gill and others in paid employment would receive salaries on top of their social wage. But they would have to pay far more in tax than now, to help meet the cost of their social wage and the social wage of those not in jobs.

This would be radically different to existing arrangements. At present Terry gets supplementary benefit, which is way below what most people see as a reasonable standard of living, on condition that he is available and willing to take a suitable job if one is offered to him. He signs on every fortnight to show he is available. This reinforces the popular notion that paid work is of central importance in life. Terry is only worth supporting if he is looking for a job. His value lies in his search for employment.

But there is more. Supplementary benefit is paid only to those who cannot provide for their needs. Far from affirming the worth of the individual, it carries an implied stigma, especially in areas where unemployment is a recent experience. It conveys the message that jobless people who get the benefit are incapable of looking after themselves. Older workers in particular tend to view it as a sign of failure. No one sees it as a reflection of their worth.

The social wage would send very different signals. Gone would be the requirement to pledge that one was available for work, and hence the implication that the unemployed are worth benefit only if they are looking for jobs. Gone too would be the means test and the suggestion that those who get benefit are inadequate. Instead, people would be guaranteed enough to enjoy a reasonable standard of living regardless of whether they worked or were unemployed. The social wage would show that they were valued unconditionally whether they had a job or not, whether they were successful at work or not, whether they were able or disabled or whatever the differences between them. Society would esteem each person so highly that it would guarantee him or her a reasonable standard of living with no strings attached. We would have moved from a work to a life ethic.

The problem is that it would be very expensive, as advocates of the social wage themselves admit. To provide everyone in the United Kingdom with a decent minimum income could push basic income tax rates up to 50 per cent or more. It is hard to imagine people in work being willing to pay that! Some might feel it was no longer financially worth their while to work. They would be likely to quit their jobs, leaving fewer people to support all those who were not working. It is not difficult to foresee the immense problems which would arise. The question is whether there are practical steps which can avoid these problems and take us at least some distance in the right direction.

WORK IS MORE THAN A CONVENTIONAL JOB

Even though work is not the basis of worth, people still want to do something worthwhile. Yet what exactly is work? If you were asked to produce a neat little package to say, 'That is work, other activities are not,' you would find yourself confronted by a legion of difficulties.

Like many people, Gill and Terry see work in terms of paid employment. Though they have never really thought about it, they have always assumed that work equals a job. Household chores such as cooking a meal or doing the washing are not work in the same sense. They are tasks to be done during leisure time. This view of work is most unfair on the housewife and others who work extremely hard but are not paid. Why should the chef be regarded as a worker, while the wife cooking the family meal is not?

When people are asked to come up with an alternative definition they sometimes suggest one like this: 'Work involves all those things we have to do to live our daily lives.' But what is necessary to live our daily lives? If someone saves part of his income for a holiday in Spain, is that necessary for his daily life? Is the definition of work to exclude that part of employment which produces income for luxuries? Are we really to suppose that in a typical five-day week, work is being in the office for perhaps three of those days but not the other two?

Others have defined work in terms of how it is experienced. 'Work is what we don't like doing. Leisure are those things we enjoy.' What about a nurse, though, who for most of her time really enjoys paid work? How is her employment to be described? So the definitions multiply, and with each there seems to be a problem. We thought we knew what work was. Put it into words, however, and it becomes more difficult.

A biblical definition

We have already seen that the Bible has something important to say about worth and work. It also has something to say about the nature of work. It defines work in an attractively sweeping way. It portrays God's work, for example, in the very broadest of terms. God's creation of the universe from nothing is seen as work.

The Book of Genesis tells us that God created for six 'days' and rested on the seventh. Educated Jews understood that the idea of God resting did not mean that he had ceased from all activity: rather he had stopped doing one particular kind of activity. He had stopped making things from nothing, but continued to be creative in the sense of keeping what he had made in existence and performing moral acts of love, mercy and compassion (as well as judgement). These moral acts were largely restorative in nature; they repaired what had been damaged.

Jesus, in a very significant statement in the Gospel of John, identifies this continued creativity of God with work. Jesus' statement was prompted by criticism from the religious establishment of his day. He had offended them by healing a crippled man on the sabbath (a compassionate act which repaired something in nature that had been damaged). The religious authorities were keen to enforce the fourth of the ten commandments which prohibited work on the sabbath.

To ensure the law was obeyed, they had tried to define work exactly. People could then know what they were allowed to do on the sabbath and what was forbidden. Some of the regulations were unbelievable. They included the provision that a person could not put vinegar on his teeth to alleviate toothache, though he could take vinegar with food. The healing of the cripple was thought to breach these regulations, and the authorities strongly criticized Jesus as a result.

Jesus' response to the criticism is most revealing. 'My Father is always at work to this very day,' he said, 'and I, too, am working.' Jesus cut through the attempt to produce a narrow definition of work. He picked up the idea of God's continued creative action after making the world, and he explicitly described this activity as work. He said that God the Father continued to work (in a wide creative sense) on the sabbath, and that he was therefore entitled to do the same. The interesting point is that Jesus defined work in astonishingly broad terms. God's work involves any act of creation – not just creating out of nothing, but keeping that creation in existence and restoring its defects.

The Bible makes clear that human work is to reflect God's work. The statement in Genesis chapter one that people are made in God's image, reflecting many characteristics of their Maker, is coupled with the idea that they rule over the world. We are given authority to 'creatively manage' the earth in ways that express God's will. The instructions to 'rule' the earth and 'subdue' it have often been taken as a licence for humankind to exploit nature mercilessly – but the terms do not mean that. Instead, they carry the idea of mastering the laws of nature. The human race is to live on the earth and master its laws. This was the original meaning of work. It is a far cry from today's popular view that work equals a job.

So when Terry was encouraged on his youth training programme to improve his skills in writing and maths, he was trying to master the laws (or rules) of these subjects. Likewise, Gill's use of the word-processor involved her in mastering the laws of that machine. Both, as far as the Bible is concerned, were engaged in work. According to the Bible, though, Gill is also at work when she is strumming the guitar in her bedroom because this involves mastering the laws of music. Equally when Terry used to play football, he was at work since he was 'subduing' the laws of physical movement.

This is a breathtaking view of work. It dissolves straight away the distinction between work and leisure. The day, as God originally intended, was not to be split between the two. Life was to be all work (or all play – they were not to be neatly divided). The only distinction God wanted to make was between work and *rest*. At work people were to concentrate on mastering the world in ways that pleased God. At rest, if people were not eating, sleeping or talking together, their focus was to shift in worship away from the world toward the Creator. Every seventh day, a day of rest, was to be set aside for worship.

Leisure had to be invented once man and woman had cut themselves off from God. As they struggled to master the universe on their own, instead of under the Creator's guidance they found that work became toil. No longer was it the joyful activity God had planned. It acquired the marks of drudgery, slog and tedious repetition so familiar today. Unable to fulfil all their aspirations in work, people had to create leisure to compensate.

The New Work Scheme

Whether or not they accept the details of the Bible's analysis, this broad view of work could be of immense significance for the unemployed. We saw in chapter one the devastating effects of boredom on the jobless, how weekdays can merge into weekends in a haze of non-activity, and how often it is only sleep which can relieve the monotony of day after day with nothing to do. People's need to be active is so great that it has been said that they should have the right to work, just as they should have the right to basic health care, education and so on.

The Bible says more than this, however. It says that work is not a right but an obligation. People ought to work, not in the narrow sense of doing things which we now consider jobs, but in the much wider sense of doing anything which involves mastering a law of nature in ways that are morally good. Clearly the unemployed cannot be expected to do this if they do not have the chance, and it would be criminal to add to their distress by placing on them an obligation they cannot meet. Ideally therefore, opportunities should be created for those without jobs to work in the Bible's broad sense of the term.

But can it be done? Can new vistas of work be opened to the unemployed? One possibility would be to set up a structured programme of activities deliberately designed to include pastimes which would not class as work in today's narrow sense, but would certainly count under the Bible's wider definition. The programme might be known as the New Work Scheme, and operate like this.

On becoming unemployed, Terry would call into the Job Centre where he would be offered a menu of activities from which he would make a choice. The selection would be as wide as possible and might include metalwork and woodwork; helping the elderly or the handicapped, or working in creches; playing one or more sports; taking part in 'outward bound'-type courses; joining a weekly self-help group; learning a musical instrument; being taught 'do-it-yourself' skills; undertaking more conventional forms of training in a Skill or I-Tech Centre; working a vegetable plot on land which would otherwise be waste; doing a first-aid course; being taught karate; and so on. Old and new forms of 'work' would appear on the list. They would be properly supervised and take account of variations of skill. Sporting opportunities, for instance, would be provided at different levels of skill according to ability.

Terry would receive advice in making his choice from a beefed-up counselling service within Job Centres. This counselling service would play a specially important role in the case of people demoralized by unemployment. It would organize, where necessary, induction courses in work for the long-term jobless. It would second counsellors to activities where there was a significant number of people whose motivation had been drained by their unemployment experience. Very often the depth of demoralization is so great that persistent care and attention from supervisory staff is necessary if the unemployed are to regain their self-esteem and overcome their lack of motivation. Counsellors would help to provide this support.

Terry is not that good with people, but he did show (if only briefly) some woodworking potential while at school. So he might be encouraged to select activities which require practical skills, and to take up football again. With his supervisor, Terry would work out a range of activites which might include learning DIY skills, tending a plot of land, joining an 'outward bound' course and playing football. Terry and his supervisor would meet regularly to iron out any problems.

Though the programme might not fill all Terry's time, it would be a great improvement on having nothing to do. It would provide some structure to Terry's week, and help to counter the endless boredom which is so unbearable. 'That's the worst part about it, having nothing to do,' said one seventeen-year-old as she described her unemployment. 'You know, just the same thing over and over again, just nothing to do.' The New Work Scheme would be a start in putting that right.

It would also give the jobless a chance to explore their abilities and find activities which gave them a sense of personal achievement. Terry might be surprised at his talent for woodwork. Though he is not the best in the class, he might think, at least he can make a better job of repairing the kitchen table than his father. His morale would probably improve and he would gradually regain not only some of the self-confidence he had lost by not having a job, but also the respect of his family. It would also provide him with company. Terry would be mixing with others on the football pitch, on the 'outward bound' course and at the centre which taught him DIY skills.

Of course the scheme would not meet everyone's needs. To a fifty-five-year-old recently out of work, it might seem more like playing at life than a real answer. But for the many younger unemployed people who have not done a lot of conventional work, it might fill the gap to some extent. And even older people might see it as better than nothing.

The community dimension

The danger, some may say, is that the scheme would promote self-indulgence. The jobless might be encouraged to enjoy themselves without any commitment to serving the community. Certainly, the Bible puts a strong emphasis on working for the community. Old Testament laws governing agriculture, for example, were so designed that the poor could share the fruits of the farmer's work. Part of the crop was to be left unharvested for the poor to gather. The land was to be cultivated for the benefit of others as well as its owners.

This emphasis on serving the community was never meant to acquire the dead-weight of moral obligation that it did in some versions of the Protestant work ethic. It was meant to be a joyful response to God's love. The biblical ideal is that service should be like an absorbing game. The players are so wrapped up in the game that they do not stop to ask: 'Am I being useful? Am I doing enough? Am I as good as the person alongside me?' What holds their attention is the joy of the game – of being fulfilled and of feeling that they are doing something worthwhile. Enjoyment and usefulness merge into a single experience.

If the New Work Scheme were to be fun, therefore, this should not be an argument against it. But Terry's supervisor would be expected to make sure that fun did not lapse into self-indulgence. He might encourage Terry to learn at least one skill that could benefit others. DIY, with its opportunities to be useful around the home, might fit the bill. In due course Terry might be encouraged to pass on his skill to others by giving a hand to those who ran the DIY teach-in centre. The supervisor would use his regular meetings with Terry to explore ways of extending the community dimension of Terry's pastimes. 'What are you doing with the crop on the vegetable plot?' he might ask him one morning. 'In what way is the community benefitting? Who are you sharing it with?'

But what about earning a living?

For people who have lost their jobs, the New Work Scheme would provide 'work after work'. It would encourage people to widen their view of work to include a host of activities not regarded as jobs today. To do this, however, it would need to jump a major hurdle. 'What's all this about new definitions of work?' Terry might ask. 'Since when has a hobby become a job? If I don't get paid for doing these forms of work, how can it be work? Who's conning who? I want a job that pays cash. You must be joking if you think that this New Work thing is a substitute for that.'

Work has always been linked with the idea of earning a living. One writer, Mark Geldard, argues that there is a fundamental connection throughout the Bible between work and maintaining one's livelihood. So, for example, after the broad definition of work in the Bible's account of creation, man and woman are told that the world they are to rule over includes what they need for food. Subduing the world involves keeping themselves alive. Any realistic attempt to extend the notion of work, then, must pick up Terry's objection and show how he could make a living on the New Work Scheme – how the opportunities for earning one's livelihood can be broadened in line with our wider definition of work.

The simplest answer would be to make a payment over and above benefit to those who join the scheme. And since we are trying to broaden the definition of work, why not call the payment a wage? Various factors would influence the level of the wage. On the one hand, the higher the wage, the more potent would be the New Work Scheme in bringing about a change in people's conception of work. Tasks which do not count as jobs today would be more rapidly seen as work if they carried a decent wage. Also, it is worth remembering that many of the jobless have low motivation at the best of times, and that long periods out of work usually leave them further demoralized. Things have gone badly for so long that they dare not hope any more. The incentive of a high wage would help to break through the despair and persuade them to join the scheme.

On the other hand, a high wage might encourage those in low-paid conventional jobs to join the scheme instead. 'That's much better work,' they might think. It would also, of course, be more expensive. Clearly a balance would have to be struck between the attractions of a high wage and the practical constraints.

Paying people to join the New Work Scheme would give the unemployed more encouragement to use their time creatively than they have at present. Instead of sitting at home doing nothing or wandering the streets aimlessly, Terry would have a financial incentive to discover and develop his abilities. Under existing social security arrangments he lacks that incentive completely. He gets the same amount of benefit whether he wastes his time or not.

The New Work Scheme would be an investment in Terry. Society would pay Terry to enjoy himself, knowing that his supervisor would encourage him to develop his potential in ways that also benefitted the community. These benefits might not be spectacular. Terry might learn how to do odd jobs around the home and for his mates; he might pass on some of hs rudimentary DIY skills to others at the centre; he might produce vegetables from land that would otherwise be lying waste. Yet it would be wrong to underestimate these achievements. Terry would be more self-confident, less ill-disciplined (from having nothing to do) and in command of a wider range of low-level skills. He would be more attractive to employers and have a better chance of getting a conventional job.

Imagine that in a high unemployment spot many of those without jobs joined Terry on the New Work Scheme. The community malaise caused by high unemployment would almost certainly be reduced as a result. The environment might become less shabby as members of the scheme put vacant land to better use. Companies would have a greater incentive to recruit from the neighbourhood since the jobless would be less demoralized. Every now and then someone with outstanding potential might be 'discovered' – a school-leaver with exceptional sporting skills perhaps; a twenty-year-old who made a go of dressmaking (thanks to the New Work Scheme) and started her own buisness; a West Indian who was encouraged to develop her musical talent. They would be exceptions, but along with the more modest achievements of others they might represent an entirely respectable return on society's investment in the jobless. They would show how plants can be nurtured from the depths of unemployment. They might give encouragement to others still trapped in the sand.

But you can almsot hear the howls that would greet the New Work Scheme (plus wage) from some quarters. The headlines in the popular press would say it all: 'Paid to play', 'Living it up on our cash', 'Paying the workshy to be even more shy', and so on. Such a reaction would be likely from those who cling to an outmoded view of work, and who would fear that the scheme could dethrone the place of jobs in our society. They would be right, because the scheme *would* challenge the notion that work equals the modern-style job. Yet what will happen if today's view of work continues unopposed? We saw in the last chapter how full-time jobs are not likely to increase by enough to provide work for all who want it. We must look for new ways of employing people.

The purpose of the New Work Scheme would be to do just that by widening our view of work. As one unemployed person expressed it: 'Instead of paid work as part of life, it will have to be work as part of paid life.' The New Work Scheme would get pretty close to that ideal. Many have called for a broadening of work, without being too specific about how it could be done. Here is one possibility. But the question remains: if it challenges such deeply entrenched views, is the New Work Scheme – with all its radical implications – a realistic option? Could it be introduced in our society, or must it remain a dream?

SHARING CONVENTIONAL JOBS

Even under the most favourable conditions, it is highly unlikely that the scheme's wages would be higher than all but the worst paid conventional jobs. There would be a limit on how much those in 'normal' jobs would be willing to pay members of the scheme. And no one would want the scheme's wages to be so high that people were reluctant to take low-paid traditional jobs which still had to be done. So at best, the New Work Scheme could only be a low paid option. It would be better than no job at all, and might be fun. But it would not be what Terry and many of the unemployed ultimately want. They do not wish to be shuffled off on to cheap alternatives. They are looking for decently paid jobs.

Again, the ideas and practices of the Bible can give us some direction here. The Bible would say that the unemployed have every right to share the decently paid jobs that are available. Under the Old Testament 'jubilee' law, in every fiftieth year land that had been sold during the previous forty-nine years was to be returned to the family which originally owned it. For one reason or another, a man might be forced to sell his property. The jubilee law was designed to prevent the family from losing that land for ever, so that property could remain more or less equally distributed between families.

Some people have suggested that the modern equivalent to land in ancient Israel is the individual's annual income, and that a radical redistribution of income through high taxation of the rich would express the principle behind this law. However, this misunderstands the law of jubilee. The law is concerned not so much with the distribution of income as with equal access to the *source* of income; not so much with how wealth should be spread after it has been created as with who should own the means of producing wealth in the first place. Because land was the principal source of income in Israel, the law was saying in effect that each family was entitled to a continuing share in society's most important source of prosperity. What was to be done with the wealth produced by the land (in today's terms, how income should be taxed) was governed by other Old Testament laws.

In our society, conventional jobs are the main source of prosperity for most people. Applied to today, therefore, the jubilee law would say that Terry and others out of work have a right not to be permanently excluded from these jobs. They are entitled to share them, just as the ancient Israelite family was entitled to a share of the land.

Avoiding piecemeal solutions

So how can jobs be shared? Some have suggested chipping away at jobs so that the bits knocked off could be stuck together to form new jobs for the unemployed. This could be done in various ways, it is said. One would be to shorten the normal working week to thirty-five hours. Another would be to discourage overtime work. A third would be to give everyone an extra week's holiday. A fourth would be to send employees on a twelve months' sabbatical every ten years. The hours, weeks or years taken from many people's jobs would combine to create the extra jobs needed to cut unemployment.

The trouble is that bits of jobs rarely combine easily to form new jobs. Imagine what would happen in the office where Gill works. She is one of five women who make up the word-processing department. Let us assume for the sake of argument that they work forty hours a week (though of course the normal week for typists is shorter than that). One day the union negotiates a thirty-five hour week. Each of the five women now works five hours less than she used to, which means that the company loses twenty-five hours of work per week altogether. What is the personnel department to do? Twenty-five hours do not equal a thirty-five hour job. So it cannot recruit another person full-time unless the volume of work goes up, and there is no chance of that, personnel are told.

Of course, a part-timer could be taken on. But since there are only five word-processors in the office, the company would have to buy an extra one, which would push up costs. To make matters worse, the machine would only be used for twenty-five hours a week – hardly the way to get the best return from the investment. Alternatively, the women might each be asked to do five hours a week overtime, which again would increase company costs, but without creating any jobs. Many firms would be likely to opt for this solution, so defeating the main point of the exercise.

If the same sort of thing happened throughout the company, total costs might rise sufficiently for the company to lose its competitive edge. Sales would drop, and instead of extra workers being hired, employees would have to be laid off. Of course, if all firms in a particular country were doing the same, the company might not be at a disadvantage against them. But it might lose orders to competitors overseas. The way to avoid this would be concerted action at an international level – a most unlikely event.

Yet even if (to everyone's surprise) this co-operation was achieved, there would still be a catch. The rise in costs would produce a certain amount of inflation. Governments might react by squeezing out the inflation in ways that created unemployment, so that relatively few people were taken off the dole overall. The inflationary danger would be especially acute if the working time was cut without any corresponding reduction in pay, which is what most have in mind when they call for a shorter working week. Costs would jump even more, intensifying the problems just described.

Similar difficulties would be encountered with limits on overtime, longer holidays and sabbaticals. The truth is that cutting away bits of jobs is too cautious an approach to create the number of jobs hoped for. What is needed is for work to be reorganized more radically. Job-sharing – dividing one job and its pay between two people – might be a more promising way forward. It is much easier to create work by splitting a job in half, with two people working part-time, than to cut off small pieces in the hope that one 'bit' can be joined to another elsewhere in the company.

Job-sharing

'That's what I need,' Gill was thinking. 'Someone to share my job.' The months had passed, she had moved out of her parents' home and had got married. Her job was helping to pay for the mortgage on the new flat. That morning though, she had discovered she was pregnant. They had wanted the baby, and Gill was absolutely delighted – or appeared to be as she told her friends in the office. But underneath the joy was the worry of how she and her husband were now going to cope financially. She would not want to go back to work full-time, she thought, but they could manage if she got a part-time job. She would miss her present job, though. All the people in her department got on so well together.

If only she could split her existing job with someone else! They might work alternate weeks, for example. That would hardly inconvenience the office, provided suitable arrangements were made to hand work over from one week to the next. Indeed, personnel might gain, Gill thought, since it would not have to advertize her job and risk recruiting a 'duff' replacement. As she thought about it, she got quite excited. 'Job-splitting's not a bad idea.' She could think of quite a few people who might want to do it – people she knew who were coming up to retirement, for example. What a good way for them to ease themselves into retirement, by sharing a job for a while.

Gill could think of other examples. There are those who want to study part-time or learn a new skill. And what about those who are planning to run their own business? Job-sharing might help them to get started, not to mention those liberated dads who want time off to see more of their children! And why should jobs only be split 50/50? Why shouldn't one partner work three days a week and the other two? And why stop at splitting jobs in half? Why not divide jobs into three or even four if people wanted?

There could be great advantages for companies if they used job-sharing to introduce flexi-time. Why not let some people contract to work thirty hours a week – ten hours on Mondays, Tuesdays and Wednesdays in some cases and ten hours on Thursday, Fridays and Saturdays in others? That way people who wanted to work thirty hours a week could do so, while the company would have people in the office or the factory six days a week instead of five. It would be much better to have individuals working different hours to suit each person's needs and the demands of the job than to have everyone working for the same fixed period. A person with a sick relative (or a new baby) could they be given the opportunity to shift from working thirty-five hours a week to working twenty hours perhaps for a few years, before going back to thirty-five.

But Gill's ideas about shared work could encounter some practical difficulties. If she shared her job and commuted every other week, she would not need an annual season ticket. But buying a weekly season ticket is quite an expensive way of travelling – would it be worth it when she was only on half pay?

And how many people really want to halve or even third their pay? Even if they did, would they really know what to do with their extra leisure time? Perhaps job-sharing is not such a good idea after all.

Job-sharing and the New Work Scheme

One way that job-sharing could be made attractive would be to combine it with the New Work Scheme. Gill might decide to share her job with someone else, working three days one week and two the next. She would then register as a part-timer on the New Work Scheme, and receive half the New Work wage. Her combined income might be two-thirds or more of what it had been previously. Her baby would be looked after in a local creche, where Gill would take turns on the duty rota as one of her tasks under the New Work Scheme.

Gill would like that arrangement, because she could see the baby regularly but would not have to spend all day with him! (When she went to work she might leave her baby in the creche provided by the company because job-sharing was so popular.) Gill's other activities on the New Work Scheme might include pottery and cooking classes. In years to come her birthday cakes might be in great demand among friends. This combination of New Work and job-sharing would be a marvellous arrangement for Gill and many others. It might appeal not only to mothers of young children and to those wanting to phase themselves into retirement, but to men and women of all ages.

It would enable them to work half-time in traditional jobs on more than half-pay. The new Work Scheme would teach them how to make use of the extra time that was coming their way as a result of technological change. And frequently they might discover that what started as a hobby became a means of augmenting their income. Though Gill might never actually sell her birthday cakes, friends would probably give her things that they had made in return.

Perhaps those who would gain most from job-sharing would be the unemployed like Terry, who would have a greater chance to share conventional jobs. Terry might go from being full-time on the New Work Scheme to being part-time on that and part-time on a conventional job – the same road Gill had travelled, but in the opposite directon. For the first time his needs of cash, company and confidence might be more or less satisfied. He might get a respectable income in activities which brought him into contact with others and in a way that made him feel good inside.

Instead of society being divided between those with the best work and those with the second-best (the 'change for the worse' picture in the last chapter) the different classes of work would be shared more widely. No elite would monopolize the plum job-work, leaving others to scratch about in side-work. Individuals would mix the two as in the 'change for the better' scenario. Changes in the nature of work would have been moulded to shape an attractive future.

If we think back to the murky water in chapter two, in which the unemployed moved from one 'trash' job to another, hoping for decent work but often sinking into the sand instead, what appears in this scenario is very different. The sharing of traditional jobs would give many of those in the twilight zone between prime jobs and side-work a crack at the more desirable jobs. It would enable youngsters to get away from insulting work which devalued them in the eyes of their mates and find jobs which had for them a degree of status.

BUILDING BRIDGES

So we have a picture of how new concepts of work might solve unemployment. But how distant it all seems! Of course it would be nice to mix different forms of work, to broaden our definition of work and to have a social security system which said that work is not the basis of worth. Helping the jobless to have access to the better-paid work, to engage in a wider range of activities alongside others and to see that work need not be the source of self-esteem would do much to meet their needs. But is this any more than wishful thinking? Are we not being transported into the realm of fantasy?

It is worth stressing that the picture is not meant to be an ideal. For many the ideal may be rather different. Perhaps they would like to see everyone working full-time on the New Work Scheme and earning much higher wages. What the picture is meant to show is the best that we can imagine for work and unemployment given the trends described in the last chapter. In view of likely changes in the nature of work, what is the most that we can hope for in the future? The answer is by no means complete, but hopefully it contains some of the key ingredients.

Presenting what is desirable is the easy bit; more difficult is knowing how to make it work. How can we make our day-dream become, if not true, at least a little less remote? How can we build bridges into the future? It is at this point that ideas for beating unemployment are often unsatisfactory. Either they are so idealistic that they cannot help. Or they are workable but unadventurous; they get so caught up by the hum-drum of the present, and so hemmed-in by concerns of practicality, that they are unable to provide the radical approach required. The challenge is to steer a course between the visionary solution and the need to make that solution work, to keep in touch both with the vision and with the reality, to be miles away in a dream but wide awake in the present. Can it be done?

CHAPTER 6

A Strategy For Unemployment

Bert was a lathe operator in the West Midlands – until 1980 that was, when his job was wiped away by a machine. The next twenty-four months were 'absolute hell'. 'That bus I used to get stops outside our house every time. Makes me ill. I ought to be on that. I ought to be on that going to work, but I'm not. Every morning I want to be on that bus outside. It makes you very bloody bitter because from starting at fourteen to finishing at fifty-three you've got nothing to show for it.' And then there are the financial worries. 'All right, at sixty-five you've got a pension, but what do you do in between those years? You're supposed to be still earning to build up for a reasonable pension when you retire, but the way it is now, knocking on for fifty-five, you're not contributing no more so your pension ain't going to be worth anything when you bloody get it.' He is not the only one in that position. 'So what are you going to do with all the people you've got in the country who aren't working?' In this chapter we shall sketch a possible answer for Bert.

It is no good coming up with proposals that are wildly unrealistic. Bert wants solutions that would help him, not marvellous theories which are quite unworkable in practice. The emphasis must be on realism, on suggestions which are technically feasible, which are likely to command widespread public support (so they will not be reversed by a future government) and which avoid weakening the economy (so pushing up unemployment tomorrow). At the same time, it is not enough to tinker with the problem. There are far too many in Bert's position for that. What is needed is a radical attack on unemployment, devised with an eye to the future. We saw in chapter four some likely trends in the future of work, and in the last chapter we considered the direction in which we wanted to mould these trends. We now need a strategy which will move us in that direction, while bringing immediate relief to people like Bert. We need reasonable means to achieve radical ends.

Here is a six-part strategy to do that:

1 Increase the rate of economic growth.
2 Increase the number of jobs created by that growth.

3 Increase the work opportunities created by those jobs.
4 Reduce the number of people wanting 'normal' jobs (but without compulsion!).
5 Reduce the unequal spread of unemployment.
6 Reduce the pain of unemployment.

The strategy starts conventionally in order to become more radical. It goes beyond the ideas of the main British political parties.

MORE GROWTH

Faster economic growth is a key to beating unemployment. Not only will it create jobs directly, it will also produce wealth to pay for other measures which have to be taken. Some people are opposed to the relentless pursuit of growth because they believe it promotes a wasteful and materialistic culture. It encourages people to see life mainly in terms of what money can buy, diverting their attention from more important values. But why not meet this objection by using growth to help the unemployed like Bert? Instead of just encouraging hedonistic patterns of consumption, economic expansion could have a more attractive goal.

Politicians on both the right and left often assume that curing our anaemic economy is *the* answer to unemployment, that getting more 'zip' is all we need. The problem with this, however, is that more growth would lead to more investment, a lot of which would almost certainly be in new technologies. According to many businessmen – and it is they who actually make the investment decisions – an increase in capital spending would produce even more situations like the one experienced by Bert.

'We saw technology coming in,' Bert said later, exaggerating a little, 'and whereas you saw one numerically controlled machine in the machine room with about 500 men, you will see about 400 of them now and no men. They can work twenty-four hours a day – three shifts, if they want. All you'll do is to switch a big panel on in the morning and let the product come out at the end.' More growth, in other words, could increase the number of jobs killed by technology, so cutting the fall in unemployment.

If this became a problem, if we were so fortunate as to experience more growth than most forecasters expect, then the rest of the chapter would become immediately relevant. The other elements of the strategy – more jobs for that growth, more work for those jobs and so on – would enable us to cope with the loss of jobs caused by new technology. They would provide a means of harnessing the extra growth to beat unemployment.

The more likely problem, however, is that Britain will not experience a dramatic spurt of growth over a long period. If we are seeking a workable approach to the jobless crisis, we need to be especially realistic about this. There are two major constraints on growth. One is inflation. Clearly the pace of growth must not be so hot that the economy lets off inflationary steam. Otherwise steps will have to be taken to cut price rises, which could bring growth to a halt. The other is the degree to which companies outsell their foreign competitors. If business is not competitive enough, orders will be lost abroad which will torpedo plans for expansion.

Overcoming these constraints is no easy matter. We looked in chapter three at four explanations of unemployment. The 'cash' view blamed it on lax control of the money supply and insufficient competition. The 'crush' view said it was due to not enough government spending on jobs. The 'change' view pointed to the lack of import controls to provide industry with a breathing-space to modernize. The 'conflict' view attributed unemployment to management and unions being at loggerheads. None of these explanations was totally adequate, though each had helpful insights. The way to get more growth would be to combine the best policy ideas to come from these four approaches.

From the 'cash' view we could take suggestions for improving competition – a 'tough' stance towards those unions which use their bargaining muscle irresponsibly, for example, coupled with an equally strong attack on business monopolies.

From the 'crush' view we might pick up the idea of a tax-based incomes policy together with price controls, to make possible a non-inflationary increase in public spending to create jobs.

From the 'change' view might come selective import controls, not to protect all industries, but new ones, in micro-electronics and bio-technology for example, which need the chance to grow and have wealth-creating potential.

From the 'conflict' view would come policies to promote a greater share by workers in company profits and decision-making, so as to increase harmony on the shop-floor.

It would need a much longer book to fill these out in detail.

This pragmatic approach would have real limitations. As we saw in chapter three, each of the policy prescriptions that flows from a particular interpretation of unemployment has major disadvantages. So against the plusses of an incomes policy, for instance, must be set the minus of less efficiency. It is worth emphasizing the existence of such drawbacks to avoid becoming too euphoric about our economic prospects.

Even so, a policy mix on the lines described could notch up the rate of growth significantly. It could make the economy a little more dynamic and create some extra wealth to tackle unemployment. That is why it is an essential part of the strategy. But it cannot be the whole strategy, because we are caught in a double-bind. On the one hand, the constraints on what we can do mean that we are not likely to get rapid growth over a long period. On the other, if we miraculously did, growth is likely to breed technology faster than jobs. In either case unemployment will remain high. What is required is a strategy that includes growth, but goes beyond it.

MORE JOBS FOR THAT GROWTH

Bert knows only too well how output in a factory can go up while the workforce is slimmed down. He is one of the casualties of that very process. It took no great leap of imagination for him to see how what happened in one factory could happen in many; how it could be true of the country as a whole. Talk to Bert about solving unemployment through economic growth (a piece of jargon that would turn him off anyway) and you would get a hollow laugh. What he wants to know is how more jobs can be created through whatever growth is achieved. How can growth be channelled to produce the maximum number of jobs?

Construction and tourism

The government can do two things: it can give special encouragement to industries which by their very nature employ large numbers of people, and it can create jobs directly itself. Two industries which prefer people to machines are construction and tourism. Studies show that the cost to government of creating jobs in these sectors is far lower than in other parts of the economy. Put another way, if government were to spend money on manufacturing industry, it would find that a much larger proportion of this cash would end up in new machinery (rather than new people) than would be the case in construction and tourism. In 1980, if you averaged the jobs across the whole economy, each job created would have required £13,600 to be spent on new machinery. In construction, however, only £5,200 per job would have had to be spent on equipment. For tourism the figure was higher, but only a little.

Goverment can build jobs in construction by extending and improving the road network, putting up more houses and encouraging energy conservation. This would be good for the economy since an efficient transport system would reduce business costs, more houses close to new jobs would make it easier for people to move to where the work was, and conservation of energy would reduce oil consumption. If Bert were to ask those who 'signed on' with him what their previous jobs had been, he would find that just over one in eight had worked in construction as bricklayers, plumbers, electricians and the like. A boost to construction would do a lot for them, and might help Bert, since fewer people would be queueing for any job he was after.

Tom Stonier, who has written an important book on the future of work, provides a small but splendid example of how tourism can reverse the spiral of economic decline leading to higher unemployment. Following World War II, the mills closed in Hebden Bridge, West Yorkshire, and jobs disappeared. By the 1960s, steady decline had made Hebden Bridge look like a ghost town. Then some local people decided to turn things around. Nestled in the Pennines, Hebden Bridge is a beautiful Victorian town, surrounded by moors and plenty of history. After restoration and repairs the town attracted tourists. Interesting shops opened and it became a nice place to live. A group of entrepreneurs moved in and opened a small factory. People with money started to move in, too, as did writers, computer programmers and commuters from Manchester. The town acquired prestige. Things had looked up, thanks to tourism.

Tourist jobs, because of the way tourism is technically defined, are created by business conferences, Disneyland-type theme parks (dubbed Mickey Mouse jobs by cynics), videos and other forms of entertainment, cafés and take-aways. Talk to Bert about the fast-food industry serving up jobs, however, and he might not be too impressed. 'Great for others,' he might say, 'but not much good for me. I mean to say, you're not going to get too well paid in those sorts of jobs, are you?' It is true that many tourist jobs are low-paid and not much fun to do, but that is the case with many other jobs as well (manual work in the health service, for instance). There are hosts of tourist jobs, though, which are not unattractive – secretaries in travel agents, to cite one example. Some, like air hostesses, have a certain glamour.

International travel, in fact, stands out like a runway beacon with its potential for growth and the ability to spin wealth, as well as jobs. Tourist spending world-wide is set for continued growth thanks to people's tendency to spend a larger proportion of their earnings on leisure as incomes rise. Government should provide large dollops of aid for tourism by giving tax concessions to entrepreneurs in the business, by paying for the industry to sell itself, and by ensuring that government support for the arts takes centre stage. In doing this they will be promoting an industry of the future. As a by-product, work-sharing, which will involve increased leisure time, may become more attractive, since people will have more to do in their spare time.

Government job-creation schemes

The second thing government should do is to create jobs directly itself. Most governments in the West have some form of job-creation scheme. In Britain, the Community Programme helped some 200,000 people in 1983/84. The programme provides the long-term unemployed with work for up to a year on projects which benefit the local community. These range from recycling wasted space, materials or resources; community education in anything from health and safety to rock music; providing services such as creche facilities and helping the elderly; providing meeting places where groups can get together in a convivial atmosphere; and producing goods through the skills and knowledge already in the community. Bert would be eligible to join the scheme because he had been unemployed for over a year. 'But what's the point?' he might ask himself. 'It would only provide work for a year. I'd be no better off at the end than I am now.'

The programme has also been criticized by people in jobs. It is supposed to encourage work which would not otherwise have been done, but this is difficult to enforce. A church needs a new hall. It has no plans to build one, so it puts one up with the help of the Community Programme. Who is to know whether this need would have become so acute in three years' time that – in the absence of the Community Programme – the church would have raised the money to pay a contractor to do the job? How can we be sure that the Community Programme team did not take jobs away from those in work who would have built the hall later? There is a real danger that the scheme is job-swapping rather than job-creating.

One answer might be to encourage partnerships between private enterprise and local government. Partnerships would be encouraged to develop projects which were not viable on strictly commercial grounds, but which might become so with public money. For example, a building company, touting for business, might suggest to the local authority that they form a partnership to turn some disused dockland into a golf course (the fastest growing sport in Britain). The project would never be viable if the company had to meet all the development costs itself, but with government help the venture could run at a profit. So under the banner of a revamped community programme, central government might fund part of the initial development on condition that the long-term unemployed were recruited to the project. Profits from the completed golf-course would go to the partnership.

For Bert this would be a great improvement on the existing Community Programme. There would be no requirement that he work for only a year. The initial phase alone of the project might take longer, and he might end up joining the golf club's permanent staff. The building firm, perhaps short of orders, would get some business. The local authority would see waste land put to good use and would share the profits. Central govenment would no longer have to pay benefit to job-seekers who joined the scheme. And those in work would have less cause to fear that jobs were being taken from them to give to the unemployed, for if the venture was not commercially viable without public funds, then in the absence of the programme it would probably not have been started. Everyone would benefit.

Small projects – turning a warehouse into a local museum for instance – might have to be encouraged first, but the aim eventually should be to promote projects on a much larger scale. We should not be afraid to think big, as the Americans did in the 1930s. Between 1933 and 1939, 3 million jobless people (about 300,000 at any one time) were put to work in forestry: planting trees; building access roads, water reservoirs, look-outs, camp-sites, log cabins; restoring historic sites; stocking ponds and streams with fish; working on pest-control, and thousands of other tasks. The creation of timber, pulp-wood for paper, fertile land and recreation areas produced untold wealth for the United States. Why should we not steam up our economic capability in a similar way? Why not make a big investment in jobs today to provide wealth tomorrow?

A middle way

These are just some of the ways in which government efforts to promote growth can be biased towards jobs. The approach avoids two extremes. It does not go as far as the large expansion of social services to create jobs which some on the left have called for. The more urgent need, given Britain's fragile economy, is to support business so that it can create jobs. Once business is thriving, we can spend more on social services, which must be an important long-term priority. A good way to help business is to back wealth-creating activities with the greatest job potential.

On the other hand, biasing growth toward jobs in ways that most strengthen the economy contrasts with the right's tax-cutting strategy. The right say that reducing taxes would boost enterprise, initiative and the willingness to take low paid jobs. It would also increase people's living standards without the need for large pay rises. Putting the break on pay, it is said, is the best way to produce jobs, since it lowers business costs, enabling firms to sell more and expand output. The right believe that tax cuts will create the most jobs in the long term.

But it is not at all clear that tax reductions would help the economy more than government spending on construction and tourism, and on job-creation projects which also produce wealth. In fact, most economists believe that spending on these lines would do more for growth than tax cuts. It would increase the country's ability to compete with foreigners (by reducing transport costs, attracting tourists, and so on), whereas a good part of any tax-cuts would create jobs alright – overseas! If people have more cash in the bank, they will be able to spend more on continental holidays, and on cars, electrical goods and the like, imported from abroad. Our competitors would be laughing.

Also, even if lower taxes did give a bigger shove to the economy, it does not necessarily follow that masses of jobs would spring from this growth. We have already seen how growth alone will not automatically produce jobs because many firms will spend their profits on new machinery rather than new men. Tax-cutters often concede this point, but say it is a short-term problem. In the long term the jobs will come. Yet as Keynes remarked, 'In the long term we are all dead.' What the unemployed want are jobs now, not after they have retired.

That is why creating jobs in ways that most help the economy is so much better. It steers midway between measures that would create jobs and little wealth, and those which would generate wealth but few jobs.

MORE WORK FOR THOSE JOBS

Even with more growth and more jobs for that growth, unemployment is likely to remain high. The jobless crisis is too acute to be solved by conventional approaches. Jobs must be shared so that more work is available for any given number of jobs. As we saw in the last chapter, a gradualist approach with steady reductions in the length of the working week would not go far enough. Something more radical is required.

Casual jobs

The first thing government should do is to encourage the sharing of casual 'here-today-gone-tomorrow' jobs. Many unemployed of course already work on the side, doing 'fiddle jobs' which stay undeclared to avoid loss of benefit. (Supplementary benefit is cut if you are known to earn more than £4 a week.) Some of the unemployed become 'dole technicians', experts at finding jobs such as window-cleaning, painting and delivering newspapers, but never declaring what they earn.

It would be wrong, however, to think that odd jobs provide an important source of income for many out of work. Research shows that odd jobs normally go to families whose heads already have full-time work – to the husband who may be a 'dual job holder' or to his wife. The cost of fares or running a van kills the moonlighting option for many jobless people, who lack the cash needed to earn the cash. Those in employment are much better placed, and are likely to hear of part-time or temporary jobs in their place of work. By contrast, many unemployed live an isolated existence, away from the job gossip which could bring employment. 'To them that hath jobs, more jobs shall be given.'

Obviously it would help the unemployed if more casual jobs were steered their way, widening their opportunities to work. This could be done by raising the £4 limit on earnings. For example, Bert might be allowed to earn £15 a week and get his full benefit on top. If he were drawing £50 supplementary benefit for himself and family, this would give him £65 a week. For every extra £1 earned for the next £15, his benefit might be reduced by (say) 50p. So if he earned £30 altogether, his benefit would be reduced by £7.50, and his total income would be £72.50 Benefit would be reduced further for earnings over £30. Bert would now have an incentive to find work, however casual, instead of the present disincentive. And there would be savings for government, if it had to pay him less in benefit.

At the same time, if it was workable, government should give a grant to employers of casual labour who recruit from the dole queue. In theory this could be done quite simply. Mr Briggs wants his house painted. A mate at work will do it at weekends for £250 'cash'. But were Mr Briggs to get an unemployed person through the Job Centre, the government might pay him £25, which would reduce the cost significantly. He would have a reason to give the job to someone out of work rather than to a person in employment. In practice, a number of complex problems would have to be overcome before a scheme on these lines could be introduced. But it would be worth trying to solve them, for the scheme might be a fairly cheap way to give the jobless a share in any casual work that was around. Against the cost of the scheme would be some savings in benefit.

More important is the precedent that would be set. There is a widespread feeling that it is outrageous that benefit rules should discourage people from looking for work. Relaxing them in the way suggested would establish the principle that it was legitimate for government to pay benefit (a grant in effect) to people who work in casual, often part-time jobs. This would make it easier for people to accept the idea that government should also pay a grant to those working part-time in split jobs.

Job-splitting

Job-splitting is perhaps the chief way in which permanent jobs could be shared. The starting point should be to offer a grant to employers and employees who split jobs. So in Bert's old factory the boss might have said, 'We won't make you redundant if you'll agree to halve your jobs, and each work half-time on a job instead of full-time.' If the workforce agreed, the company would have received a government grant for each split job, as would employees who took part in the scheme. The grant in effect would be society's way of compensating employees for the lack of the full-time, permanent work they had been brought up to expect. For Bert, this option, though not as good as a full-time job, would be considerably better than the dole.

Instead of seeing job-splitting as a way to avoid redundancies, another company could use it to reduce local unemployment. Employees would be offered the chance to share their jobs with someone on the dole, each person working half-time. Priority might be given to 'lads of the dads'. Again the government grant would be paid to the company and to both halves of the job pair. Though not as good as a full-time job for the unemployed, it would be better than no job at all and might lead to full-time work later.

The British government already offers a grant to employers who split jobs, but the scheme has had little impact. This is partly because the rules of the scheme have deterred employers and partly because there has been no grant to employees. Paying a grant to employers *and* employees is vital. Change must be nurtured with financial incentives, not left to sprout spontaneously from the soil of inertia. Because for many people job-splitting is such a novel form of work, even with government grants it will take time for the scheme to catch on. Meanwhile, Bert remains out of work, waiting...waiting...

So, to speed up the splitting of jobs, the scheme should be targeted at, and sold hard to, groups to whom it could have a particular appeal. The elderly approaching retirement, for example. They could be offered part-time pensions if they split their jobs. The government announced in early 1985 that grants would be paid to both employers and employees where jobs are split for people approaching retirement. This was a step in the right direction. But it is unlikely to have much impact because the age qualification is too narrow, not enough is being done to market the scheme and it has not been presented as part of an overall strategy. Good ideas lose impact if dribbled out on a small scale without any apparent relationship to each other.

Young people who join the scheme could be offered free training (plus grant) during the non-working part of their week. Those wanting to set up in business with the security of part-time work behind them might be offered financial help if they split their jobs. The scheme could be gradually broadened (as funds allowed) until it was open to everyone. Once it was well established, other flexible work patterns involving the sharing of jobs could be encouraged. For example, a grant might be given to groups of five people who worked four days a week instead of five, creating one extra job.

Some people are sceptical about job-splitting. They believe that two into one won't go, not least because the unemployed want whole rather than part-time jobs. Yet in a 1982 survey, almost half those without work expressed some interest in job-splitting while a quarter were interested even if pay was no more than the dole. Sixty per cent of the jobless in Britain are single, which means that in 1984 they were entitled to a maximum of £26.80 a week in supplementary benefit. Half a job plus grant would give them considerably more, even after tax. 'I'll do it,' said one person out of work, 'if it's the difference between having a job and not having a job.'

Other people doubt that job-splitting would be attractive to employers. There is no doubt that it would make supervision more difficult. But against this and other problems would be the government grant; more intensive work by job-splitters because they would be working shorter hours; greater job satisfaction resulting in lower staff turnover and absenteeism; the potential for one half of the pair to provide cover while the other half was on holiday, off sick or on a training course; and the opportunity to introduce new shift arrangements. If there were enough volunteers, job-splitters might be encouraged to work three days each week so that the office or factory could be kept open till Saturday instead of closing on Friday.

We stressed in the last chapter the need to avoid a two-tier society in which an upper layer monopolized well-paid jobs while the bottom went without. Job-splitting would help to prevent this. If one in ten vacancies was filled on a job-split basis, up to 300,000 people could be taken out of unemployment. A quite significant move would have been made towards sharing prime jobs among those who wanted them.

REDUCE THE NUMBERS
WANTING CONVENTIONAL JOBS

The first half of our strategy was designed to increase the opportunities to work by more growth, more jobs for that growth and more work for those jobs. It might be that Bert would find some employment as a result of this, but there is a good chance he would not. The numbers out of work are so large that realistically, after doing everything suggested so far, many will remain jobless. The next part of the strategy – reducing the numbers wanting conventional jobs, reducing the unequal spread of unemployment and reducing the pain of unemployment – is therefore designed to make the best of a bad situation. Given the shortage of work opportunities, what can be done for those who would like to work if they had a chance?

Cutting the number of people in or looking for normal jobs would give the unemployed a better chance of getting work. Many people believe that a smaller national workforce is inevitable. They expect it to be 'topped and tailed' as young people spend longer in education or training and older workers retire earlier. People will not start work till they are twenty or so, while the retirement age will fall steadily to fifty-five.

But achieving this by a compulsory squeeze on both ends of the working life would be far too autocratic. It would reduce the individual's freedom to work or not, instead of extending it, which is what most people want. A more attractive approach would be to widen the choice for individuals of every age. At present, people often want conventional jobs because they have no alternatives.

Providing new options for those in jobs or seeking them would create space on the workbench for some of the unemployed. People who want to work would have more chance to do so.

Training

One way to do this would be to expand greatly training and re-training opportunities. If tourism is a growth industry of the future, so too is education. New technologies are creating demands for all sorts of new skills. The advance of bio-technology is hampered by a shortage of qualified staff. Computer programmers are continually having to update their expertize. The need for new technical skills is cropping up day after day. Then there is the expansion of the tourist and leisure industries which will put a premium on people skills. Hotels, airlines, travel agencies and others who provide quality customer service will be the ones on the roller-coaster ride to wealth. It is commonplace to say that the single life-long skill is a thing of the past. As skills become obsolete at an accelerating rate, the demand for training and re-training will grow.

Meeting the demand will create jobs in itself – jobs in training, adult education, the production of education materials and so on. Training will also take people out of their jobs or out of their job-hunt for a while. Eventually everyone who wants to train or re-train should be able to do so. But as a first step, the training and work-experience provided to unemployed school-leavers under the Youth Training Scheme should be extended to all sixteen to nineteen-year-old job-seekers. It is important that this expansion does not reduce the quality of the scheme by spreading scarce resources too thinly. Already there are complaints that the scheme is considerably below par in some places. So perhaps expansion should start in the areas of highest unemployment. Increasing the reservoirs of skills might encourage companies to locate in these areas, providing extra long-term jobs, while more training would reduce the horrific level of youth unemployment.

This extra training should not be compulsory. Least of all should we aim, as some suggest, to eventually exclude all teenagers from jobs so that they are either at school, or in further education or in a YTS-type training scheme. Many young people are fed up with school. If they have not been very successful, they will be keen to shun a situation that carries even the faintest reminder of past failure. They are likely to resent compulsory extra training because, however well presented, it will almost certainly appear like school. If trainee allowances are set well below youth wages (as is present practice), many will see the compulsory training as an excuse to reduce teenager's pay and will resent it for that reason too.

It is worth remembering Bob Taggart's experience with American youth training programmes: you can take a person to training, but you cannot make them train. Some groups, like Project Fullemploy, which work with the unemployed in Britain, have found the same. They find that they have to allow trainees to drop in and out of their schemes – to go on 'walkabouts'. This is not true of most youngsters on the Youth Training Scheme, but the warning is there. An extension of compulsory training to cover *all* young people not at school or further education could produce trainees who are uncooperative, who continue patterns of truancy started at school, or who drop out altogether. Employers who provide the training may become disillusioned and withdraw from the scheme, leaving government with the problem it had at the beginning – what to do with young people who cannot get proper jobs.

It is vital, then, that additional youth training be voluntary. It must also lead somewhere. Teenagers often see training schemes as a 'con' because they do not end in a job. They suspect that the schemes are society's way of washing its hands of youth unemployment – of kidding the kids. The reality in high unemployment spots is that for most school-leavers, training is a break from unemployment, not a solution. At the end of the great temporary fill-in, the route to a permanent job is as blocked as it was before. To meet this problem, those completing the scheme might be given first pick of job-split vacancies or of places on a revamped community programme (if no other jobs were available). Giving priority to those who finished the course would reduce the incentive to drop out, as would an increase in the trainee allowance for individuals progressing through the scheme.

A voluntary programme, with maximum choice and variation in training and work-experience, would look less like school. Ensuring that it led somewhere would make it seem less like a stop-gap. Instead of narrowing opportunities by excluding all teenagers from jobs, options would actually be widened. Those who found paid work could take it; others could choose between school, college, university, a youth training scheme, or periods of 'holiday'.

Caring in the community
More and more people are saying that where possible we should care for the elderly, handicapped and ill within the home rather

than in large, impersonal institutions. The quality of care is often better, and most people feel more comfortable at home than in 'alien' surroundings. Britain's Social Democratic Party has called for a 'Carer's Charter' in which a grant would be paid to all who stay at home to look after a dependent relative. There are strong employment reasons for moving in this direction as fast as we can afford. Though the number working in 'institutions' would fall as a result, this would be offset by an increase in professional support to carers at home.

If the grant was pitched at a decent level, a number of people might find that caring for relatives at home was more appealing than sorting biscuits all day or working in a stifling, hot laundry. Leaving jobs for paid work in the home would create work opportunities for the unemployed. Particularly if the grant was called a wage, it would encourage people to see that home-based activities were as much work as employment outside the home, so widening the popular view of work. It would also be a small step toward improving the status of housewives – that major group of unwaged workers whose problems are still too often ignored. In parts of North America housewives describe themselves as Domestic Resource Co-ordinators! Let's hope that this is a sign of a higher status to come.

Voluntary early retirement

Many older people stay in work because they have to; they need the money. If this need was reduced, quite a few older workers would be willing to retire early, creating employment for someone on the dole. An extreme idea is that we should move to compulsory retirement for people in their late fifties, say. But a compulsory twenty-year retirement (or more in some cases, as people live longer) could become an elongated fag-end to one's life. The elderly may have little to do or feel little valued. What started as a solution to one problem would be likely to cause another – a crisis of the old.

Far better to encourage flexible retirement, so that people can choose when to retire between the ages, for example, of fifty-five to sixty-five (ideally, fifty-five to seventy). A fairly cheap and quite effective way of working towards this is Britain's Job Release Scheme, known as the job swop scheme. Men over sixty-four receive a government grant if they retire early and their employer hires someone out of work. The scheme has proved quite popular. If eligibility were extended gradually to everyone over fifty-five, well over 100,000 extra people might take advantage of it.

Put this alongside job-splitting for older workers, and you have the making of a new deal for the elderly. Instead of going straight from work into retirement at sixty-five (or sixty for women), which was the traditional pattern, they would have a greater range of options. They could choose when to retire between fifty-five and sixty-five, and whether to phase themselves into retirement by working part-time for a while. Tackling unemployment can benefit those in work, too.

REDUCE THE UNEQUAL
SPREAD OF UNEMPLOYMENT

In chapter two we saw how the burden of unemployment falls on particular groups, which are often concentrated in the 'inner city' with its shabby streets, closed factories and demoralized communities. No one can imagine that a complete solution exists to the swathe of desolation that has cut through many areas of urban decay. But there are plenty of things which could bring hope.

A stronger bias in unemployment measures toward the 'left-behinds', as they have been called, would be a start. A number of schemes could be implemented first in areas with the highest unemployment, only later being extended to the country at large. It is worth bearing in mind, though, that residents in these areas tend to have a low estimate of their own worth and ability. Having been constantly at the receiving end of decisions made outside their communities, they feel at the mercy of forces beyond their control. The weighting of unemployment schemes to the left-behinds, therefore, is likely to reinforce existing feelings of dependence since once again they will be relying on outside support. Additional measures are needed to help these communities to help themselves.

Inner cities

Perhaps the best hope is to reverse traditional approaches. On the whole, attempts to attract companies to the inner city have not been conspicuously successful. Forces which destroyed the old jobs have been too strong to combat. Why not work with the grain of social forces rather than against them? Attempts to improve the inner city environment must continue, of course. But given that firms prefer to locate away from the inner city, might it not be better to take people to the jobs instead of bringing the jobs to the people?

This could be done by adopting a modified version of the

American 'affirmative action' programme. The programme was introduced in the late 1960s to encourage the employment of ethnic minorities. If Cranco Engineering sells goods to the Federal Government, it must show that it has done its utmost to get an ethnic balance in its workforce similar to that of the surrounding community. So if 1 per cent of blacks in the neighbourhood are accountants, 1 per cent of Cranco's accountants should be black too. If it cannot find people with suitable skills, it must set up a training programme for local blacks. The programme need not cover the company's whole range of skills: it would be enough to focus, say, on the training of black secretaries. Companies normally choose to provide training in skills which they particularly need, making it likely that trainees will get a job and that the firm's own requirements will be met. The programme has been highly successful.

Importing it would be a good way to improve job prospects for Britain's minorities. However, the different culture of Britain makes a white backlash against favoured treatment for minorities likely. This could be so strong that race relations would be severely damaged. To avoid this, the scheme could be modified to apply to high unemployment spots rather than specific ethnic groups.

Take a firm within commuting distance of one or more unemployment disaster areas. It would be required to show that its workforce reflected the proportion of the city's population in those spots. The company might find that the residents were not qualified. It would then have to show that it had set up a training programme for them and made reasonable efforts to attract them to it. If Bert lived in one of these areas, he might say that the cost of travelling to the outer city was too high. Government could overcome this by subsidizing the fares of those travelling to work from areas of high unemployment.

Making unemployment disaster areas places of opportunity in this way might well win public support. It would kill two birds with one stone. It would assist spots with the highest unemployment, but also help ethnic minorities in a non-racial way. Because minorities tend to be concentrated in places with the most acute unemployment, they would be given better access to the jobs they need. There is a good chance that this would not increase racial tension (always a danger with special measures for ethnic groups), since whites would have no grounds for complaining that they were being discriminated against. The scheme would be 'colour-blind' – whites in high unemployment spots would be covered too.

But business would be likely to object, as it did at first to the

American programme. On a visit to Washington I was treated to a brilliant account by a senior figure in the Reagan Administration as to why he thought 'affirmative action' was bad for the economy: it distorted market forces. But when I asked what business thought, he replied, 'Gee, I just can't understand it. They seem to love it.' The reason I discovered from business leaders was that the programme enabled them to help minorities in a way that also met company needs for skilled labour. Having first hated the programme, firms had come to see its advantages. It represented a typical American combination of conscience and self-interest.

Opposition in Britain might be overcome by proceeding cautiously and by giving financial incentives to firms which co-operated. A first step might be to give a handful of progressive companies the financial incentive to mount pilot affirmative action schemes in selected areas. The results, if successful, could be used to publicize the virtues of the programme, while any lessons to be learnt would influence the development of a national scheme. Business co-operation with a national programme might be encouraged by tax concessions, discussed below. Once affirmative action was well under way, however, companies would be likely to reach the same conclusions as their American counterparts. Far from being a drag on the economy, in all probability the programme would be seen as an asset.

Regional policy

Many high unemployment areas are in regions where the jobless total is generally high. If the unequal spread of unemployment between regions is not reduced, the proposal just described will merely share out the misery in regions where the misery count has already reached exceptional heights. So affirmative action, British-style, needs to be complemented by an active regional policy. There should be three prongs. The first should be to use public money to stimulate business activity in depressed regions. This is being done in various ways, ranging from grants to attract companies into these regions, to the use of 'pump-priming' money which will catalyze business ventures. There is plenty of scope for reinforcing this first prong. In 1984, the British government announced a substantial cut in its regional budget.

Second, new ways should be explored of attracting firms to job-starved regions. One shortcoming of regional policies has been that companies have been attracted to these regions with grants to cover the cost of plant and equipment. This has skewed development away from creating jobs to buying machines. Where a company has had the choice of two factory processes, one employing more people than the other, there has been a strong temptation to go for the latter, so as to get a larger government grant. This skew, however, should be greatly reduced from 1985 as a result of a change in government policy.

One way to make regional policies still more people-based would be to follow another example from the United States and offer training grants to companies willing to invest in the region. Imagine that Fulton Engineering wanted to open a factory in Bradford but found a shortage of electricians there. It would be encouraged to arrange for the local technical college to mount a special training course specifically tailored to the company's needs. The cost of the course would be met by central government. Such an approach would be a quite radical innovation for Britain and would have to be phased in over a number of years, but it has been most effective in parts of the United States.

While the first prong is short term and the second medium term, the third is distinctly long term in nature. Publicity has been given to the success of 'science parks' in the United States. These comprise business ventures designed to exploit advances in university research – in bio-technology, for example. Ventures have mushroomed in places like Boston, Massachusetts, producing jobs as a result. Science parks are being tried in Britain, too, but so far with less success.

Government should weight increases in the funding of academic research toward high unemployment regions. These regions are often well endowed with high quality universities and polytechnics – in Glasgow, Manchester, and so on. Indeed, education is among their chief assets. It makes sense to build on this as far as possible. In particular, government should give generous grants for projects in those regions designed to bridge the academic world of research and the commercial world of product development. The aim should be to take a leaf out of the American professors' book and encourage an amoeba-like development of new companies, each feeding off the others and starting up new enterprises. Beside creating a certain number of jobs, these high-tech firms would create the wealth to help regenerate the local economy and underpin the other strands of regional policy.

It might then be possible to stem the massive haemorrage of skills from regions where unemployment has been acute for many years. The better trained and educated have moved to where the jobs are, leaving the least skilled behind. This in turn has discouraged firms from building factories and offices in regions which need the jobs most. Reversing the process would make these regions more attractive to companies and encourage the creation of jobs. With affirmative action lifting unemployment high spots by spreading work in the regions more widely, the burden of unemployment would become just a little less unfair.

REDUCE THE PAIN OF UNEMPLOYMENT

The question for those still unemployed, after government has done all suggested so far, is how to reduce the yawning gulf between the quality of life in and out of work. How can we move towards the ideal of the social wage, for example? The attraction of the social wage is that it expresses the key principle that work is not the source of human worth. People have such immense value whether they work or not, that they are worth being guaranteed a reasonable (rather than subsistent) standard of living irrespective of whether they have a job.

Work and worth

For Bert, who feels rejected, signing on seems to confirm that he is no good. Hanging around while he registered for the first time conveyed a hidden message: society does not consider the jobless worth the cost of providing a better service. The pittance that represents Bert's dole sends a second message: 'You're not worth anything more.' The obligation to sign on every fortnight sends a third: 'A job is central to life. You ought to be looking for it. We refuse to pay you if you're not. And we can't trust you to look for it if you don't renew your commitment every two weeks.' Bert can only conclude that he must be inferior. His conclusion is reinforced by the means-test for supplementary benefit – a test in effect of whether Bert is good enough to provide for his family.

The social wage is far too expensive to introduce straight away. But the present system in Britain could be improved in three stages – by raising benefits, then reforming benefits and finally replacing benefits. To raise benefits, the one-year earnings-related supplement to unemployment benefit, which was phased out after 1979, should be restored. This would bring unemployment benefit during the first year out of work closer to previous earnings. Those who have been unemployed for a year or more should receive the higher long-term rate of supplementary benefit, which they do not get at present, even though it is paid to other long-term claimants such as the sick. If Bert was claiming supplementary benefit for himself and his wife in 1984, the higher rate would have been worth some £11 extra a week. This is no mean sum when you are on about £50.

These two measures would make a significant dent in the poverty of job-seekers. We have seen how lack of cash adds much to the pain of unemployment – how it makes it difficult to keep up social contacts and stay busy, so undermining one's self-esteem. There is of course the problem that the higher the benefit the smaller may be the incentive for the jobless to find work. On the other hand, the softer the financial cushion of unemployment the more comfortable it will be for people changing jobs. A greater willingness to switch jobs, instead of clinging to outmoded working practices, will produce a more dynamic and prosperous economy which will create jobs in the long term. The two arguments probably cancel each other out. Why not give the unemployed the benefit of the doubt?

Raising benefits can be done straight away. Reforming them would take longer. Yet in the framework of the existing system, it is possible to think in terms of two important changes. The first would be to reduce sharply the number of jobless people who draw supplementary benefit either because they are not entitled to unemployment benefit, or because unemployment benefit is not high enough to support their families. Receiving unemployment

GETTING THE BENEFIT
What British claimants received in May 1983

Receive Unemployment Benefit only
24.9%

Receive Supplementary and Unemployment Benefit
8.8%

Receive Supplementary Benefit only
53.7%

UNEMPLOYMENT OFFICE

SOCIAL SECURITY

Claim benefit but receive nothing
12.5%

Source: *Unemployment Unit Bulletin*

rather than supplementary benefit would avoid the stigma of having to prove that you are unable to provide for your family. It would also avoid the shock of finding that your thrift in the past disqualified you from supplementary benefit because your savings were too large.

This change could be accomplished by:

☐ Paying unemployment benefit to those who have been out of work for over a year.

☐ Raising the level of unemployment benefit by restoring the earnings-related supplement and making it payable for more than a year. (Previously, payment stopped after twelve months.) This would reduce the need to augment unemployment with supplementary benefit.

☐ Making unemployment benefit payable to all who have been working or just left school, rather than only to those who have paid enough contributions. Often the jobless are not entitled to unemployment benefit because they have not paid enough 'stamps'.

The second reform would be to alter the rules for signing-on. After the jobless have registered for the first time, there is no real need to continue signing-on. Since benefits are now taxed, the Inland Revenue will 'notice' when a person has returned to work. A person wanting to earn sums hidden from the taxman or benefit office is likely to do this whether he signs on every two weeks or not. In those areas where unemployment is still a stigma, the jobless could be spared the fortnightly reminder of their failure to get a job by stopping the requirement to sign on regularly. If this is too radical, a first step might be to reduce the frequency of signing on to once a month (and perhaps arrange for it to be done by post or through the local Post Office). Benefit office staff would then have more time to improve the speed of service to people registering for the first time, and to run a new programme along the lines of the New Work Scheme.

In the much longer term it may be possible to replace the benefit system altogether with arrangements more akin to the social wage.

Turning leisure into work

Tom is an out-of-work graduate. He is one of the more fortunate unemployed because he has a number of hobbies and is well motivated. But even he found that being jobless meant that 'you've got nothing driving you and nothing to push you. It's all too easy to drift into being around the house saying "I'll do that tomorrow." I think leisure ought to be organized. Work's organized – there is a distinctive pattern there. There should be some way to structure people who haven't got jobs into doing things. If it's left to the individual he won't do it.' The New Work Scheme would achieve this. The question is how to move towards it.

Fortunately, important precedents have already been set. The Sports Council, as well as individual clubs, are promoting sporting activities among the jobless. The Youth Training Scheme includes some unconventional forms of job-training – an 'outward-bound' course, for instance, for which trainees receive an allowance. Work on the Community Programme includes many activities suggested for the New Work Scheme in the last chapter: helping the elderly, providing facilities for people to develop their hobbies, and so on. A wage is paid to those on the programme.

Stepping toward the New Work Scheme would require a fairly simple development of concepts within the Community Prgramme and Youth Training Scheme. Activities under the Community Programme could be extended to include more in the way of sports and hobbies, on the grounds that this was training as understood by the Youth Training Scheme. Instead of just providing leisure for others as is often the case now, members of the programme could be encouraged to engage as part of their 'training' in the leisure pursuits themselves (for which they would be paid). Activities open to them could be steadily widened, and in time perhaps the one year limit for staying on the scheme could be extended. All this would have to be done gradually to avoid losing public support. The time spent on projects benefitting the community, for example, might be slowly reduced, allowing – bit by bit – more time for pastimes of greater enjoyment to those on the scheme. Members of the programme would continue to be paid a wage, as they are at present. It has been said, rather unkindly, that the British take their leisure at work. If these steps were taken, one day the unemployed could find themselves at work during leisure.

Eventually the existing Community Programme would disappear. Part of it would become an American-style New Deal Programme, involving partnerships between local authorities and private enterprise. This would create more jobs out of economic growth. The other part would evolve towards the New Work Scheme. The aim would be to encourage the jobless to structure their time creatively, to take them out of life in a void. It would also give them a better opportunity to develop their abilities. Rather than merely reshuffle the pack of cards they already have, they would have the chance to deal themselves a better hand. Voluntary groups would play a major role under the scheme, providing opportunities for community and 'self'-service.

Great care, however, would have to be taken that the community service dimension did not become a way of replacing, on the cheap, provision by local or central government. There is no point in improving one person's unemployment experience by taking work from someone else.

Indeed, introducing recreational activities into the community programme would reduce the risk of the programme competing with those in jobs. Participants would be increasingly engaged in totally new forms of 'work', which threaten no one. There have been calls to extend the programme to all the long-term unemployed – over 1 million of them. These calls would make sense if a 'new work' element was introduced into the existing programme and slowly expanded. There would be less chance, then, of a vastly extendly programme poaching work from people who already have it.

Put it like this and some may think, 'how obvious and easy.' That is precisely the theme of the chapter. There are plenty of simple steps which taken together could have a profoundly radical effect on work and unemployment. Paying people to do sports and hobbies (as well as serving the community) would help to broaden the popular view of work, especially if the payment was called a wage. Once the New Work Scheme was well established, it could be linked with job-splitting to provide people with a mix of different kinds of work. They would do better-paid prime jobs for some of their time, and lower-paid (but perhaps more interesting) forms of work for other periods. We could avoid a future in which some hogged the best-paid jobs, while others made do with the second-rate.

Company involvement

The New Work Scheme would be quite expensive, which means it would have to be introduced slowly. Again, priority should be given to areas with highest unemployment. There is one way, however, to increase funds for the scheme. Some have proposed that government should pay a grant to companies for each person they recruit who is out of work. It is thought that this would be a good way to tackle unemployment since it would encourage firms to take on extra labour. But the proposal is likely to be quite wasteful, since payments would be made to companies who would have recruited the jobless whether the subsidy was available or not. If a retailer is short of twenty staff, there seems little point in giving him a subsidy to hire people he would have taken on anyway.

However, it might be possible to give the subsidy to employers who paid for places on the New Work Scheme. A grant equal to what it costs government to keep each person on the dole might be paid to companies for every individual they sponsored on the scheme. Imagine that a large employer had to close one of its factories. Meeting the cost of a number of places on the scheme would enable him to put something back into a community reeling under the loss of a major source of employment. Unions might find it was worth while to negotiate such arrangements into redundancy agreements. Spurred on by the unions, combinations of business and government money might enable the New Work Scheme to expand quite rapidly. Our aim – is it too much of a dream? – should be that one day all the unemployed will have the chance to join the scheme if they want.

MAKING THE STRATEGY WORK

The important thing about tackling unemployment is to have a strategy that is comprehensive – that will ensure that the needs of unemployed people are met at least in some way. In the case of the strategy sketched here, Bert might get a full-time job as a result of more economic growth or the creation of more jobs for that growth. He might get a half job or a casual one because the unemployed have more opportunities to work for any given number of jobs. He might be helped by a reduction in the number of people wanting job-work, or by a reduction in the unequal spread of unemployment. If he is untouched by all this, the bottom line is a reduction in the pain of unemployment. It would be difficult for Bert to slip through the net and be left where he is now.

Getting business co-operation

It is one thing to have a strategy, quite another to make it work. Much of this strategy depends on business co-operation: in forming partnerships under a New Deal-type scheme, in splitting jobs, in making 'affirmative action' work and in sponsoring places on the New Work Scheme. If companies failed to respond (despite the offer of government grants), then however good the schemes are on paper they will make little difference in practice. Companies must be persuaded to play their key role in beating unemployment.

Government might do this by saying to business leaders, 'We want you to set up a company to market our schemes to business. It's much better for you to do this than us because companies are more likely to listen to a fellow businessman than to a civil servant.

If you do this and sell our schemes vigorously, and if we see that business is making a positive response, then we will reduce company taxes by (say) 1 per cent. But,' government might add, 'if business fails to respond we might have to raise company taxes to pay for alternative unemployment measures. If we do that, we shall look at ways of exempting firms which have played their part.' This should ensure business co-operation.

How could we pay for it?

There remains the biggest question of all: how is government to pay for what could amount to a very expensive set of proposals? Part of the answer is to note that most of the proposals could be phased-in. To start with, they could be targeted at specific groups of the jobless, particularly in unemployment high spots. Later they could be broadened to include others who are out of work. This would keep down the initial cost. The question then becomes: how can government pay for the schemes to be introduced on a sufficiently large scale to have a major impact on unemployment?

The easiest answer would be to pay for the strategy through faster economic growth. That is why growth is so important, if we can get it. But even with slow growth the rest of the strategy is still feasible, provided money can be found from other sources. A second answer, then, would be to make savings on other government budgets (defence?) and to push for some EEC cash. Realistically, though, the amount that can be 'raided' from these sources is likely to be small. So a third possibility would be for government to increase its borrowing. Many experts believe there is scope for this without damaging the economy. Borrowing an extra £1.5 billion a year (what many think is modest) would pay for measures covering perhaps 500,000 jobless. But if the extra borrowing raised interest rates, we would have to set against this some loss of jobs as companies decided to postpone investment.

Finally taxes could be raised – and for good reason. It is outrageous that those in work should have tax-breaks while the unemployed are broken by poverty. Restoring the 3 per cent cut in income tax made in 1979 would raise about £3 billion. If all this were spent on unemployment schemes it could help between 1 and 1.5 million people. (This assumes no change in benefit levels, though.) If those in jobs tried to recoup their lost tax in higher wages, however, there would be some offsetting decline in jobs. Higher wages would make it more difficult for companies to compete with overseas firms, forcing some workers to be laid off.

Even so, there seems to be plenty of scope for helping the jobless by raising taxes. It is an option that does not tax credibility. For, according to a survey in 1983, 74 per cent of the British public would have been willing to pay an extra 1p in income tax to provide the necessities for all. Thirty-five per cent would have been prepared for an additional 5p – £5 billion in all which would pay for a massive onslaught on the problem. The difficulty in tapping this goodwill lies in persuading people that something can be done. There is a great malaise. Many think we are powerless to produce effective solutions to unemployment.

It was this pessimism which largely enabled the Conservative government to win the 1983 general election. As one of the party's strategists recounted, 'Our attitude polls... showed that a substantial number of voters did not blame high unemployment on the government. They blamed it on historical factors and on the world recession... This told us that we did not have to be over-defensive about unemployment. We could emphasize the historical factors and the world recession and it would strike a chord. It worked. People voted "to continue as we are". They thought unemployment was inevitable.'

It is not. Much can be done about the problem. Realistic but very interesting solutions exist. Though they might not provide a total cure, they would at least set us on the right course. They would make unemployment less high, less unequally distributed and a less painful experience. It would be lower, fairer and better. They would also help to shape the future in ways that would benefit society as a whole. Surely that is worth paying for, is it not?

CHAPTER 7

Local Action

In May 1982 a group of friends and neighbours in Pallion, Sunderland, met to discuss a redundant local factory which used to employ 2,000 people. After its closure the year before, the factory had been stripped and vandalized. The residents were upset by this waste, concerned for the safety of elderly people living near the factory and keen to improve facilities in the area. The meeting elected two housewives, a former ward councillor and the local vicar to see what could be done.

One of their first steps was to ask Sunderland's 'War for Work' campaign for support. Their idea was to turn the 84,000 square foot factory into training workshops, a nursery, and office and factory units. These would create jobs, allow space for exhibitions and communal services for local businesses, and provide leisure facilities in an area which had few. They hoped that the project would act as a springboard to new, small enterprises and help to rebuild community spirit.

Expert advice from the local council, financial support from a variety of official sources (not to mention several companies) and masses of hard work made it possible to launch a company with 500 shareholders, all living in the Pallion area. The shareholders receive no profits from the company, but each has a say in how the company is run. The aim is that the company should have genuine local roots. All too often factories are shut by head offices miles away from the people devastated by the closure.

By 1984, Pallion Residents' Enterprises Ltd had set up, under the government's Youth Training Scheme, a training workshop for over thirty young people who specialized in engineering and new technology skills. Space had been converted to house a computer co-operative for thirty disabled people. The factory units were nearing completion, and local residents were showing great interest in renting them for small businesses. Plans were afoot for a multi-purpose sports area to occupy the centre of the building. There seemed a real possibility that eventually all aspects of the development would create 300 jobs directly, and that knock-on effects would produce a good number of additional jobs. Much had been achieved in a short time.

STARTING OUT

Pallion Residents' Enterprise is just one example of the hundreds of local initiatives that are mushrooming in response to unemployment. They are launched by tenants' groups and community associations, by trades councils and women's groups, by councils of voluntary services, rural community councils and information and advice centres, by churches, by community centres and neighbourhood centres, and by other voluntary groups. They vary greatly in what they do, but they have this in common: individuals have been stirred by the agony of unemployment to do something about it.

Small beginnings

It is easy to write off the importance of what these groups are trying to do. For those interested in big solutions, it is tempting to sneer at initiatives which seem so miniscule against the massiveness of unemployment. After all, what are 300 jobs against the 2,000 lost in Pallion? Often it does seem that gigantic efforts, on a local scale, do only scratch the surface. Some people go further and say that local action can be positively harmful. People may mistake it for *the* solution to unemployment, whereas in practice it barely touches the problem. The public's conscience is numbed, which allows the politicians to sit comfortably on the crisis instead of rousing themselves to do more about it.

This is an important point. It is no good pretending that local efforts can be a substitute for well-designed national policies. Government action is vital if a large hole is to be made in unemployment. That is why we have looked at government policies first. However, small outcomes are no reason for being small-minded about local action. If you have a job, imagine being out or work yourself. The loneliness, boredom and financial hardship of unemployment may force you to do something. 'It's all very interesting about what government can do,' you may think. 'But what can *I* do? I can see the problem in the street. I'm affected by it myself. Surely I don't have to sit back and wait for government to act? I might have to wait ages! I know I can't make a big impact, but isn't it worth doing *something?*' It is better to help a few people than none at all. And better to work together, in voluntary groups where there is strength in numbers, than on one's own.

A second reason for local action is that far from reducing popular demand for government initiatives, the exact reverse can happen. Many voluntary groups have found that working with the jobless brings wider issues to the surface. Applying for government cash often highlights some of the ways in which government policies close down opportunities instead of opening them up – for example how strings attached to government grants restrict what can be done. Members tend to become more aware of some of the other effects of government policies, such as the way social security regulations disadvantage the jobless. They frequently conclude that a different and more urgent political approach is required. At the same time, people in jobs may see or hear about local initiatives, think and talk about them, and move the jobless crisis up their agenda. Local action can therefore increase awareness of the political dimension and encourage more informed discussion of what government should do. The more local projects there are the greater this effect.

Local action also provides an opportunity to try out new types of work. Many groups working with the unemployed see themselves as innovators of a new life-style, pioneering ways to live outside the confines of the traditional job. They hope that what is grown on the seedbed today will blossom tomorrow. After all, great movements in history have always started small. Who had heard of the peace movement in 1978? Yet a few years later it was a major force in world politics. May it not be that local experiments with the unemployed will suggest new ways for society to express the view that work is not the basis of worth, work is not the same as the traditional job and that prime jobs are not to be monopolized by a few? Indeed, might not local action be the way to create a 'phoenix economy' out of the failure of the old? These are optimistic sentiments perhaps, but they are better than the resigned acceptance of community decay.

Overcoming lethargy

It is no simple task to galvanize a group into action. Where unemployment is not especially high, there may be apathy because of ignorance. People cannot be concerned about something they do not know about. If they have never been without work, or don't have friends or relatives out of a job, they cannot be expected to know what unemployment is like. Only when they have the facts can they decide whether to be troubled by them. In high unemployment spots, despair may be more of a problem. People may be genuinely concerned about unemployment, but be thoroughly confused. They may not know what to do or where to start. They may feel powerless, imagining that the situation is so hopeless that whatever they do will make no difference. Lack of self-confidence is often a major stumbling block.

A member of a voluntary group who wanted to do something about unemployment might start by asking for a chance to share their concern with the appropriate people in the organization – perhaps a standing committee. Having prepared carefully, they might describe briefly what it is like to be unemployed, give a few choice facts about the problem, such as the number out of work in the area, and ask permission to form a group to examine what (if anything) should be done. The group could help to overcome any ignorance or confusion which existed. It could be formed straight away, without alarming the more cautious that they were being bounced into something without proper thought. The group might be asked to report back after six to nine months.

Involving the jobless

It is vital to start with the right attitude. There are people who think in terms of doing something *for* the unemployed, but that is a patronizing approach which fails to give the jobless the dignity they deserve. It must be action *by* the unemployed or *with* the unemployed, but not for them. Making this a first principle will give concrete expression to the idea that the out-of-work have worth regardless of whether they have a job. They must be treated accordingly, as genuine partners.

In practice this means that from the start groups looking at the possibility of local action should include at least some people without work, who can help the group to focus on the genuine needs of the jobless. Some groups at the initial stage are composed entirely of the unemployed. This can have the advantage of encouraging members to focus for a while on their own feelings of frustration and anger. Expressing these can be a cathartic process which prepares the group for the next stage of its work. If feelings are bottled up, they may be expressed in ways that disrupt the group later on. Resentment at not having a job, for instance, may be vented on another member of the group.

If people are involved in planning groups to help the unemployed and none of the members are jobless, it is worth asking why not. What does this say about the motivation of the group? Is it more concerned about its own needs than those of the unemployed? Does its exclusiveness reflect attitudes in the organization that it represents? Does it suggest perhaps that the organization is not very accepting of the unemployed? And might this not be the place to start – to make contact with local people out of work and draw them in?

FINDING OUT

How long a planning group spends on collecting the facts, and what facts it considers worth collecting, again says a lot about the group's motivation. If its basic aim is to use the out-of-work to meet the needs of the organization, then it will not spend too much time finding out about unemployment. It will concentrate from an early stage on practical questions such as sources of finance. Once these have been answered, the group will go out in a blaze of glory, having done its bit for the unemployed in a way that met the organization's pressing needs for the gardens to be tidied, the creche to be manned, the walls to be painted and so on. Scarcely a thought will have been given to who will benefit most – the unemployed, the wider community or the voluntary organization. No one will know because no one will have asked the jobless what they want. The vulnerability of the unemployed, already exploited in the job market, will have been exploited once again.

Assessing needs

The introduction to *Action on Unemployment*, a directory of 100 projects with the jobless, notes how description of 'drop-in' centres reveal the disappointment often felt by organizers who have set out with the best of intentions. Those with experience of these centres advise, '"Do not impose things on the unemployed from on high", "ensure that the unemployed express a definite need for the project", "be willing to work with the unemployed in their own locality", and so on. There are laments over despair, lethargy, feelings of worthlessness... Too many of us assume that we *know* on behalf of others, and are surprised when the others vote with their feet when offered the fruit of our arrogant decisions.'

This is a useful reminder that plenty of time should be spent gathering information about unemployment in the neighbourhood. The sort of questions worth asking are:

☐ What unmet needs does a person out of work have?
☐ What are the different groupings among the jobless? How do their needs differ? Are some groups more needy than others?
☐ What are other organizations in the area doing to meet these needs?

☐ Where are the gaps? Which groups of unemployed are getting least support?

☐ How big a problem is unemployment in the locality? Is it more acute elsewhere? (The group may eventually decide that it should support action in an area of greater need).

☐ What expertize or sources of information are available locally which would help us to be better informed? Some useful sources of information are listed at the end of this book.

☐ Are we sure that we have done enough to understand the problem?

Discovering resources

Obviously at the finding-out stage it is also vital to discover what resources can be drawn on to launch an initiative with the unemployed. What financial support is available? The main sources of possible help can be found at the end of the book.

Looking at some of the funds available may spark off a debate about how much to rely on government support. Sometimes people adopt a surprisingly uncritical approach. They want the money but they forget about the conditions, which is a great mistake. Government money does not come without strings. It is important to examine these strings carefully because they can tie down a project in damaging ways. A good example is the one-year limit for individuals to stay on the Community Programme. This produces agony as participants leave after twelve months, often with no job to go to. 'Are we really in the business of providing only temporary relief?' is a question that may need to be asked.

Under many government schemes, groups have to apply for a renewal of financial support each year. This can be time-consuming and the project may suffer from uncertainty about whether the application will succeed. Long-term planning becomes impossible. Sudden changes of policy at the centre, such as reduction of available funds, can frustrate or destroy local initiatives that have taken ages to plan and launch. Many groups have found their objectives thwarted by government's refusal to fund under the Youth Training Scheme any training that includes political ingredients. Training, for example, in how to be aware of broad social issues is not allowed. Difficulties like these have encouraged some to urge a 'leave well alone' approach to government schemes.

But following this advice would drastically reduce what voluntary groups can do with the unemployed. Three-quarters of the projects listed in the *Action on Unemployment* directory made use of government funds. They suggest that a pragmatic approach of using government money, but with eyes open to the constraints this imposes, can be made to work. It is worth noting, too, that some government schemes do have redeeming features. The Community Programme requires work to be done on projects which benefit the community. This enshrines the idea of socially useful work. Employed imaginatively, the scheme can provide an opportunity to pioneer tasks not seen as traditional jobs, so widening the popular idea of work.

The 'Impasse' centres are an excellent example of this. One of the people involved in Impasse asked, 'Can the jobless, deprived of status, herded into dole queues and fitted into numberless forms of bureaucracy, really pioneer a new life ethic?' Impasse is determined to demonstrate that the answer can be "yes": and that it is on behalf of all of us and in advance of all of us that the unemployed will develop new work values, etc, unrelated to money, and new lifestyles not based around paid work.'

Self-help is the essence of Impasse. At its Middlesbrough centre it provides a woodwork shop, craft-rooms with silk-screening, sewing and many other crafts, and a garage where vehicles can be serviced and rebuilt. Tools can be borrowed for use at home and skilled advisors are at hand. Besides a drama group, a sports league is being set up to include football, chess, table tennis and darts teams who will play against other groups of unemployed people. During the holidays there is a computer camp, to which parents can come with their children to learn more about computers in an informal atmosphere. Craft camps on the same lines are being established.

Impasse has its roots in a small initiative launched in the late 1960s by Bill Hall, who worked for the Arts and Recreation Chaplaincy in the north east. By 1984, with centres in Middlesbrough, Redcar, Skelton Thornaby and Spennymoor, and a full and part-time staff of twenty-nine, Impasse had grown way beyond Hall's original dream – a good example of how small beginnings can have unexpectedly large results. Its Middlesborough leaflet boasts, 'Here at "Impasse" people are discovering skills they didn't know they had'. The negative experience of unemployment has been turned into something positive. Because there are few alternatives, Impasse has been forced to rely heavily on the Community Programme to finance its staff. Yet despite the strings attached to the programme, the project has evolved in a highly imaginative way. Clearly it has been better to make the best of a bad job than to leave in the cold those with no job.

Besides information about finance from outside bodies, the group will need to think about its own resources. What can the organization it belongs to provide in terms of buildings, skills, money and time? It is important also to discover sources of technical advice (about planning regulations, employment law and so on). Much can be learned, too, from talking to others involved with the jobless locally and by finding out what is going on further afield. This will help to avoid mistakes and unnecessary duplication of effort, and may suggest ideas for what should be done. While the members of a planning group will start with their own ideas about the type of project they want to recommend, it is important to keep an open mind to what is happening elsewhere and to new possibilities. It would be a pity to settle for second-best because the group was fixed on its own ideas.

Counting the cost

'Recognize that it will take a great deal more energy than you think.' 'Problems involved vandalism; underestimate of staff and finance required; local people unclear of project's purpose and have a general feeling of worthlessness.' Comments like these underline the importance of counting the cost before launching an unemployment project. It is far better to recognize the difficulties before one starts, than to be disappointed later on. Better in fact not to start at all than to withdraw when the going gets tough, leaving disillusionment and bitterness behind. Talking to others is the best way of discovering the problems.

It may then be helpful to ask these cautionary questions before going further:

☐ Do you get discouraged easily?
☐ Could you cope with waiting, lack of money, endless set-backs, opposition, bureaucracy, apathy and despair?
☐ Are you willing to take risks?
☐ Have you thought about the time involved?
☐ How big a priority is this? Does it fit into the aims of the organization?
☐ Can and should these aims be changed to accommodate work with the jobless?
☐ Are you willing to make mistakes and learn from them?
☐ Are you consistent?
☐ Are you willing to assess and reassess the situation and your own motivation?
☐ Can you work with others whose philosophy of life is different from your own?

☐   Are you willing to consult, co-operate and co-ordinate with others?

☐   What is more important to your organization: small insignificant things, or making an impression? Giving or getting? Serving or being served? People or property?

THINKING OUT

By the end of the finding-out stage, a planning group should be able to define the needs of the different groupings of the unemployed in the area, give those needs priorities, list what others are doing (are priority groups receiving priority attention? Have lower priorities been left so far behind that they have now become a priority?) and identify ways that their particular organization might get involved. The next task is to think out what should be done.

Setting aims

It is important that the group be clear about its aims. Does it want to be a catalyst spurring others into action? Or does it want to work mainly with the unemployed themselves, helping them to meet their needs? Can or should it do both? If it wants to work with the jobless directly, which group or groups of the unemployed should it focus on – the old or the young? Men or women? Those with families? The long-term jobless? Ethnic minorities? Clearly some of these may overlap, but it is worth remembering that some unemployment groups have fallen apart because they try to reach too wide a variety of people.

Having settled on a target, the group must then decide which needs to address – needs for company, for information and survival skills, for something to do or for cash? Should an attempt be made to combine several of these? Finally comes the question of how these should be met. Should they be met in a fairly conventional way, or in a way that seeks to pioneer new attitudes to work and lifestyle? Should local business ventures be promoted, for instance, or new forms of work?

Setting aims will determine the type of action the group researches. There are many possibilities, the first of which is to support projects in another area.

Help for groups in another area

'Think globally, act locally' is a good motto for any voluntary group. It might be specially apt if, for example, one belongs to a church in an area of comparatively low unemployment. The church may be keen to help the jobless in its own neighbourhood, and there may be much it can and ought to do. But a look at the wider horizon may show that the scale of their problem is a fraction of its size in other places. They may also see that they have one thing that many poorer churches desperately lack – the cash to pay for basic facilities, or that vital staff member to work with the unemployed. For some inner city groups the salary for just one person can be the difference between starting a project and doing almost nothing at all. Sometimes the best way an affluent church can support the jobless is to support financially those working in areas of highest unemployment. It is all too easy to look after one's own, to the neglect of those in greater need.

This raises painful questions about priorities. Should the top priority be to tackle unemployment in the surrounding community or in localities where the problem is more acute? Is it possible to do both? If a commuter-belt church, for instance, decides to support an inner city congregation, it will then need to think hard about the nature of that support. Will the support foster a paternalistic relationship between the two churches or a genuine partnership? 'Left-behind-communities' have had their self-confidence and resourcefulness sapped by years of depending on others. At the very least therefore, outside financial support should have no strings attached and be on a long-term basis. The receiving community can then decide and be responsible for how the money is spent. Being able to plan ahead, knowing that the money will be there unconditionally, will enable the community to take greater control of its own destiny.

Help for groups in the same area

The People and Work Unit in Newport is an independent organization that encourages local economic and social enterprise. It has done what it describes as 'action-research' projects on topics such as 'Women and Work', 'Health and Unemployment' and 'Community Business.' It has organized seminars on the issues and designed and sponsored a symposium on 'Community involvement in local economic developments' which was funded by the EEC with participants from all over Europe. There is a library and a regular review of social and economic issues in the region.

This is one example of a group which seeks to encourage others to do something about unemployment by increasing public awareness of the problem. Other groups with a similar aim have made contact with local schools to discuss how school-leavers are being prepared for life in a community with few jobs. Still other groups have brought local employers together to encourage them to help the jobless. There is no reason why a 'catalyst' should not organize a pre-redundancy course to be made available to employers on demand. The course might include sessions on 'signing on', 'the job hunt', 'government unemployment schemes', 'state benefits', 'managing money' and 'finding things to do'.

There is an important task to be done in getting employers, trade unions, education bodies and other interested groups together to look at future skill needs in the area, and to see how local training schemes can be co-ordinated to meet them. Lack of planning and foresight is a major reason for skill shortages. The Manpower Services Commission gives financial support to 'local collaborative projects' on training.

Help in making the best of no job

Most voluntary groups concerned about unemployment prefer to work directly with the jobless rather than to encourage action by others. To help the unemployed make the best of not having a job, some have set up 'drop-in' centres which can have a variety of aims. They can be a refuge where people meet and make friends free from pressures of home, the street and officialdom; a source of information about social security rights, housing, recreation and so on; a place where the jobless can find someone who will listen to their problems and help to work out solutions; a centre with facilities for people to cook a cheap meal, do their laundry or mend their clothes; an opportunity for people to relax, play music or take part in sports, drama or discussion.

The Green Lane drop-in centre in Nottingham was opened in September 1980 by a committee made up from the Probation Service, Social Services and the Leisures Services Committee. Marriage tensions, wife and child battering, alcoholism, depression, bad debts, petty crime, and ultimately the break-up of families alogether prompted them to try to ease the difficulties of jobless families. At first the centre was not a great success, but football proved to be the answer. By playing footall together in a league sponsored by local businessmen, the group of players began to work as a team. They asked for a members' committee to be set up at the centre, and are now planning a workshop with facilities for woodwork, welding and silk-screen printing. If all goes well it is hoped to turn this into a community co-operative with profits being used to benefit the neighbourhood. This is a good example of how drop-in centres can provide opportunities for the unemployed to come up with ideas which are more imaginative than the centre's original vision.

The trouble is that in many cases centres never get beyond organizing things *for* people who are out of work. Feelings of dependence are reinforced since the jobless are encouraged to think 'I'm only good enough to be on the receiving end'. Drop-in centres can become drop-out centres, as one person put it. Because of this, many prefer the idea of the self-help group made up of unemployed people and run *by* them. These groups typically start as 'tea and chat' groups, meeting once or twice a week. But as relationships cement and confidence builds up, some move on to develop a range of sporting, cultural and leisure acitivities. Other groups set up unpaid Neighbourhood Work Teams to decorate the homes of the disabled, shop for the elderly and so on.

Still others organize skill-swap schemes. In Wales, the Cwmbran skill-swap has a full-time co-ordinator who checks any jobs that people need doing against a list of available skills. One person may agree to look at someone's broken washing machine, another to baby-sit. Jobs are not done on an exchange basis - baby-sitting in return for mending a washing machine. Rather, all jobs are done free as straight gifts. The washing machine will be repaired, even if the owner cannot pay the person back. This has got over the government's objection that 'direct job-for-job' swapping was too much like paid work, which means loss of benefit. It also avoids the problem, which has bedevilled other job-swap schemes, of finding a person who wants something in return for something another person has got. Needs and skills cannot be matched so neatly. The willingness of people to help each other without being helped in exchange makes the scheme fairly unique, and reflects the strong social unity of the group.

Drop-in centres and self-help groups have had a mixed response from the jobless. For Jenny, an unemployed graduate, 'having the confidence thing is important. You get more and more pessimistic about applying for things and you do feel a lack of confidence about your ability to get a job. It helps having people there who are in the same boat, to make a joke about it rather than them feeling failures because they'd never got anywhere.' But for forty-two-year-old Harry, without a job for eighteen months, 'I think that sounds utterly boring to me – just to sit there and I'm telling you my trouble and you're telling me your trouble. That wouldn't help. I'd feel worse.'

It seems that these centres are least successful where relatively few are out of work. The jobless want to be treated above all as normal people. In places with low unemployment, drop-in and self-help centres frequently convey the idea that the out-of-work are a 'separate breed' who need special treatment. The unemployed will tend to avoid them like the plague. But where it is more socially acceptable to be without a job because of the large numbers in that position, self-help groups and drop-in centres often receive a warmer welcome.

Help in getting the skills for a job

A number of self-help groups provide basic training for their members – anything from building skills to numeracy and literacy to computing – in the hope that this will help people to get a job. Many have made use of government schemes, notably the Youth Training Scheme in which the voluntary sector plays an important part.

If a group wants to develop a training project, it will have to decide who it will be for. It should also ask whether it wishes to reinforce existing patterns of skill or whether it wants to promote healthier ones. Does it mind strengthening the training bias toward white men, for example, or does it want to address the special needs of women or blacks?

The Bristol Women's Workshop aims to teach women skills traditionally regarded as male. It provides woodwork tuition in a way suited to women's needs, as well as home maintenance skills such as plumbing, mending a window, replacing a lock or wiring a plug. Many would not have considered attempting these skills in a mixed setting, but find it less intimidating to be taught by women tutors in an all-female environment. Training women in 'male' skills will improve their chance of getting better jobs, so reducing the odds against them at work.

A standard objection to training projects is that they are a bridge to nowhere. Because of the job shortage, trainees are unable to get work at the end. Learning with little prospect of earning can be a thoroughly demoralizing experience which leaves trainees less inclined to get much out of the course. This eventually affects the organizers and instructors who lose interest themselves. The quality of the course then suffers as it becomes a steadily inferior 'fill-in'. Much better, it is said, to have action which tackles the root of the problem.

One resonse to this very important objection has been to include 'survival' training on the course to help trainees cope with life when they have finished. This at least tries to grapple with the problem, even if it is not much of an answer. The Bristol Women's

Workshop has a notice board which lists people requiring help for all sorts of practical jobs. Women completing the basic course are encouraged to do these jobs, frequently accompanied by a tutor to oversee the work and to give support. This is fine for the women, but may mean that someone in work who would have done the job misses out. One person could be helped at the expense of another, a common problem with action on unemployment. An alternative solution may be to provide opportunities for trainees to form a self-help group and possibly to do some voluntary work after the course is over. This is far from ideal, but at least it is something.

Help by making extra short-term jobs

Many action groups try to provide the unemployed with temporary jobs. These are usually financed by government under schemes like the Community Programme, and often aim to benefit the community. Driving the elderly to day centres, running a counselling service for people made redundant, turning waste land into garden plots, and converting a disused warehouse into an arts centre are all good examples. *101 Ideas for the Community Programme* is a useful thought-starter for those wanting to explore the possibilities.

Projects run with government money are normally required to create work which would not otherwise have been done. This is to avoid taking one person out of the dole queue by pushing someone else in. How conscientiously groups try to meet this requirement shows whether their main concern is to tackle unemployment or to meet their organization's immediate needs. Often groups try to bend the rules by providing 'on the cheap' work which the organization would eventually have paid for anyway, so risking the job of someone already in employment. This turns job-making into job-taking.

For a group thinking about a possible project it may be helpful not just to ask 'do we have any plans for doing the work now?' but 'are we ever likely to have plans for doing it?' It could be that while there is no money for an extra gardener at the moment, deterioration of the grounds will force the organization to hire one eventually. If that were to happen, using government money would not create a genuinely new job. Work would be taken from the person who would have done it later.

Temporary work schemes are often criticized for being palliatives. People may stay on the project for a year, at the end of which it's back to unemployment with no more chance of getting a permanent job than they had before. To meet this objection, some groups have designed projects which both serve the community and provide training in skills which are in local demand. A community secretarial service could give training in office skills while providing typing, duplicating, minute-taking and mail-out services for local groups. A community newspaper could offer training in design and graphics, layout, printing, photography and writing skills.

Another possibility is to encourage ex-teachers and others within the voluntary body to pass on their skills even if this is not required under the government scheme. Monday afternoons might be spent on training in how to play a musical instrument, in numeracy and literacy, or in whatever other skills are on offer. Even if the training is unrelated to the rest of the project's work and proves little help in getting a permanent job, it will at least enable participants to improve their abilities. It might leave them better placed to survive, and find something to do, during a subsequent spell without work.

Alternatively, members can be encouraged to meet regularly as a group when their time on the project is over, and they can be given opportunities for unpaid voluntary work. These might help to fill the void of returning to unemployment. Or else a group could ask a major local employer to give preference to suitable candidates from the project when taking on staff. The project would then become a genuine bridge between unemployment and a permanent job (though of course others, not on the project, would have less chance of being recruited). These are just some of the ways in which temp work can be made less of a dead end.

Help by making extra long-term jobs

Many groups consume a lot of energy trying to create permanent jobs, which they see as an attack on the root cause of unemployment. Proper work is being created, they feel, rather than fill-in hobbies or temp jobs. Initiatives come in a huge variety of forms. Some focus on encouraging self-employment. One church (appropriately called 'Hope') supported two young women while they established their own painting and decorating firm.

Young people working for STANDBY in Chatham, Kent, do cleaning, decorating and gardening jobs. Under an agreement with the local office of the Department of Health and Social Security they can claim social security provided they remain available for full-time employment, and 'work' for less then twenty-four hours a week. They are not allowed to earn more than £4 a week if they are drawing supplementary benefit, or £2 a day on unemploymen benefit. But – and this is the important point – they can earn 'credits' for the work they do. These credits are then saved until there is enough to meet the cost of tools and equipment for self-employment ventures, or the cost of specialized training. It is an ingenious way of getting round the earnings limit on those drawing benefit, so that people can acquire what they need to strike out on their own.

Other groups, as in Pallion, have converted disused buildings into small workshops for the jobless with woodwork and similar skills. Financial support for budding entrepreneurs is available under the government's Enterprise Allowance, provided applicants have £1,000 in capital. Enterprise trusts have mushroomed, formed normally by a consortium of companies, the local authority and voluntary groups. They seek to co-ordinate help and advice available locally for entrepreneurs who want to start a business but need a hand to hold. Another approach is to develop business ventures which are owned by their members, previously unemployed, on a co-operative basis.

The Facility of Art and Craft Enterprises Ltd, based in Glastonbury, is an ambitious attempt to combine training with the creation of long-term jobs. The training, largely financed through the Youth Training Scheme, is available in up to 140 skills: travel videos, costume and portrait dolls, candlemaking, cheesemaking, scenery making, sheepskin products, shoe-making and musical instrument restoration, to name but a few. Trainees are placed in workshops where they take part in all the practical commercial and decision-making aspects of the business, learning skills of promotion, publicity, office work, designing, marketing, delivery and maintenance. They are then encouraged to set up on their own, which is the job-creation aspect of the scheme, and their products are promoted locally and nationally through FACE's large gallery, 'Workface'. This attempt to revitalize the craft industry is a healthy reminder of some of the 'new' forms of work likely to spread in the future.

FACE may seem rather grandiose to a group which is strapped for resources and unsure of its ability to take any form of local action. But its ideas can be scaled down. Imagine that several churches or voluntary groups in an area were willing to work together. Between them, they might find a number of people (housewives, perhaps) with different art and craft skills. It might be possible for each of these 'experts' to teach their skills to a small group of unemployed young people. With financial help under one or more of the government's unemployment schemes, the churches might find that they could pool their resources and set up a small shop to sell the finished products. The range and quality of products could steadily grow as the young people developed their skills, possibly one day setting up their own small businesses. Fostering art and craft skills may be especially appropriate in rural communities, many of which are no less hit by unemployment than the cities.

What looks impossible to a group on its own can seem much less daunting when several groups work together. Groups may have to create the structures which enable them to collaborate, but often these structures exist already. In the Anglican Church, for example, local churches are grouped together in 'deaneries'. Sometimes there is little practical co-operation between these churches. A joint unemployment venture could be just what the structure needs to come to life.

An important issue in job creation projects is ownership. Conventional partnerships, in which the partners hire their employees and take the main decisions, can avoid mistakes by putting control in the hands of those most able to exercise it. But this is not always appropriate. Peter Raynes is the founder of 'Instant Muscle' – originally a Surrey-based group of youngsters who work on a co-operative basis to do small household repair and maintenance jobs. According to Raynes, the group 'started as a partnership employing other people. But it gave employees no sense of belonging, of doing their own thing. The whole point ought to be to get depressed unemployed young people to realize that there are things they can do for themselves. They just looked on the partners as bosses, and that was hopeless.' 'Instant Muscle' only took off when it became a co-operative.

A third possibility is the 'community business', owned by individuals outside the venture but living within the locality (though capital may come from government or private companies). Profits are ploughed back into the enterprise. Pallion Enterprises is a case in point. The aim is to give the community a chance to express its involvement in job-creation. But it is often difficult to get much local support.

Another issue is the possible conflict between the venture's social and commercial aims. This has been a particular problem for Wastechaser, a Teeside company which provides work for young people with special difficulty in finding and holding jobs. It collects waste paper on behalf of a paper merchant from 20,000 households, used clothing on behalf of Oxfam, and aluminium foil and drinks cans for sale to a local scrap dealer. One of the organizers reports, 'If Wastechaser was a purely commercial venture, the company would not employ as many staff. Although there is a hard core of very reliable workers, there is a high turnover of people who are unable to work steadily over a period. Eventually they leave – we do not dismiss them.' It is important to be clear about priorities.

The biggest danger of all is that Peter will be robbed of a job to creat one for Paul. For instance, a cycle repair shop may create three jobs. But by doing the work more efficiently than its rivals, it may destroy four other jobs in town. A furniture repair business may create five jobs, but take work from two people making new furniture because fewer people need to replace what has broken. A large-scale expansion of voluntary help in the community may encourage the local authority to cut back its welfare services. (There are reports that this has happened.) Immense efforts have been spent on local job-creation ventures, too often with little thought as to how many old jobs have been destroyed in the process. Once again it is vital to be clear about what you are doing.

If it seems that creating jobs will destroy old ones, there may be a case for exploring other options. An exciting – if demanding – possibility would be for employed members of a voluntary group to consider whether they could share their jobs, so that they had more time for their voluntary work. One or two people, if they knew a person out of work, might pair up with them and urge their bosses to let them work their jobs as a pair. Though at present the opportunities for job-sharing are limited, there is much to be said for exploring whatever opportunities exist. Showing how people in work can share their jobs with the unemployed would point a way in which society ought to be moving. It would ensure that genuinely new, if part-time jobs were created.

Help by making brand new kinds of jobs

One of the objectives of CATS (Leeds) Ltd is to encourage people to explore unwaged work. Workshop facilities are being provided so that the jobless can express their own creativity without necessarily making any money. This is seen 'as an alternative to waged employment and not a second-best'. The aim is to show that creative work, rather than money, is central to a person's self-fulfillment. But the trouble with unwaged projects is that people find it very hard to see them as work. As we saw in chapter five, work *includes* earning a livelihood. In practice, real commitment may not come without pay. Some community projects have run aground because an unpaid worker has not put in the time he or she should.

If local action is to help widen the notion of work, therefore, it is not enough to engage in activities that are not usually classed as jobs (new forms of communal work, sport, etc.): these activities must be paid. Is it too visionary to hope, for example, that a church will one day launch a project involving the jobless in a mixture of hobbies, sports and community service for which they will receive a proper wage – a tiny version of the New Work Scheme in which a person might be paid to do tapestry, shop for old folks and learn tennis, for example? Is it conceivable that members of that church, or of a 'twinned' church in a more wealthy area, would meet the cost of those wages?

One possibility, learning from the experience of STANDBY in Chatham, might be to allow members of the scheme to earn credits so that they remain eligible for supplementary benefit. (Of course, this would need to be cleared with the local social security office first.) Once the credits had mounted up, they could be used by individuals in many ways: to provide the capital to qualify for the Enterprise Allowance and become self-employed; to meet the cost of a training course; or to find a job away from home. The innovation, however, would be to pay these credits not just for fairly conventional forms of work as is the case with STANDBY, but for a much broader range of activities along the lines of the New Work Scheme. The project could be started on a very small scale, in keeping with the limited resources the church had available.

Such an initiative would be a means of eventually freeing the unemployed to stand on their own feet instead of reinforcing their dependence on others. Perhaps its biggest plus is that it would create genuinely new work rather than traditional 'job-work' which may already be done by others. The risk of taking a job away from one person in work to give to another out of work would be greatly reduced. The project would give concrete expression to the idea that work does not equal a conventional job. It would be a sign of what tomorrow could be like, a laboratory experiment in broadening the concept of work, a trial run at the future for the surrounding community to watch.

Summary

So there are many forms of possible action. They include:
- [ ] **Help by working through others** (help for groups in another area; help for groups in the same area).
- [ ] **Help by making the most of existing work opportunities** (help in making the best of no job; help in getting the skills for a job).

☐ **Help by expanding work opportunities** (help by making extra short-term jobs; help by making extra long-term jobs; help by making brand new kinds of jobs).

Often several of these options can be brought together in one scheme – as has happened in many of the examples quoted. Help in getting the skills for a job may be combined with efforts to create jobs for those who complete their training. Self-help groups to enable the unemployed make the best of no job may also provide some kind of training.

LAUNCHING OUT

Having started out, found out and thought out, the next stage is to launch out. This requires an effective management structure involving people with knowledge of (and some standing in) the local community, people with relevant expertise (of working with volunteers and of legal and financial matters) and people who understand unemployment (including the jobless themselves). Maria Pernatta, the director of a large community scheme, has given this advice: 'Muster a small-being-beautiful organization committee of people who are totally committed to the project envisaged and who have first-hand knowledge of running a business. Anything less will experience every pitfall in the book. If necessary, 'buy in' the business skills.'

There are pitfalls in negotiating with government bodies, in getting planning permission, in meeting the requirements of employment law (on health and safety, for instance), in handling money, in giving adequate support for full-time staff and in a host of other areas. Having experts will help to avoid disasters. People with thorough knowledge of the social security system may also suggest benefit 'wheezes' like the one used by STANDBY.

Sometimes local businessmen can arrange for companies to second managers for a period, which can be extremely helpful. But there are dangers. It can provide firms with a golden opportunity to get rid of incompetent staff! Also, a manager who knows his way round a large, rather bureaucratic company, may be less at home in the informality and ad hocery of a voluntary group. So it is worth checking out any generous-looking offers of help.

Those thinking about some form of local action may find it helpful to read *Beating Unemployment*'s seven case studies of how projects were launched. It is vital, too, to consult widely at every stage – with planning departments, other organizations in the field, relevant experts and so on. Letting others know what is going on will help to ensure that local resources are used as effectively as possible. If people are not told, some activities may be duplicated while gaps are left in other areas. Keeping members of the voluntary organization informed will ensure that commitment to the project grows and that available material and other support is forthcoming.

Criteria for a new project

One thing is certain. Practical constraints will produce a project which is far from ideal. One must simply do the best one can. As a group wrestles with the disappointments and frustrations, it may be helpful to keep in mind criteria for judging the value of an unemployment project. Every so often the group might go down the list and ask, 'How far are we meeting the criteria? Can we do any better?'

Frequently the need to compromise and the temptation to settle for second best are so great that it is easy to forget what the project should be achieving. Checking the list can spark the group's imagination. So maybe a compromise is necessary – there is no money to pay members of the scheme a wage. Is it possible to compensate by rounding the project out in another direction? Can the training element, for example, be made better still?

It is amazing how many groups seem to launch initiatives without seriously considering what makes a good project. They think it is sufficient to decide on a scheme and find ways to start it. But it is crucial to realize that this is not enough. A clear idea of what represents a good project will spur the groups to be more ambitious and to go the second mile.

Researching the plusses and minuses of different projects will soon suggest criteria for a good one. The following will almost certainly appear on the list.

A good project will:
1 Benefit the community in some way. Obviously job-seekers want to do something worthwhile.
2 Teach a *recognized* skill. If that is impossible it will do something to develop the potential of participants (training in 'life skills', for example).
3 Involve work that would not have been done by someone in a job.
4 Lead somewhere. If the project does not provide a permanent job, there will be follow-up opportunities for those finishing the project (voluntary work, a self-help group, and so on).
5 Encourage activities which can be done in the company of others to counter the cruel isolation of unemployment.

6 Increase the income of the jobless. If that is impossible, at least there should be advice on how to make benefits go further and on how to get all the financial support one is entitled to.

7 Include in its leadership people who have been or are unemployed. Then the jobless will be encouraged to take responsibility for their lives and not passively receive services given by others.

CHECKING OUT

Unfortunately many planning groups believe the task is done once the project has been launched. It is important, though, to keep track of the project and make sure it is achieving its aims. Every so often the project should be carefully reviewed:

☐ How well is it meeting its objectives? What problems have still to be solved? Can other groups suggest ways of making the project more effective?

☐ How valid are the original aims? Are other groups meeting them better than we are? Is this a reason to set ourselves new goals? Have new and more pressing needs arisen within the community?

☐ Have we become too content with second best? How many criteria for a good project are being met? Should we be pioneering new forms of work and income-sharing? How complacent are we?

It goes without saying that job-seekers on the project should take part in this review. If it is a project *with* them and not just *for* them, then they will have been involved at every stage – from starting out to finding out, thinking out, launching out and checking out. Ideally it should become their initiative – a local example of how new opportunities can grow from the anguish of unemployment.

KNOCKED OUT?

One clergyman from an inner city remarked that the average inner city church (or voluntary group) with limited resources might find this chapter rather daunting. They might feel overwhelmed by some of the large projects described, knowing that they could never scale such heights. Or they could be put off by all the problems they might meet – each option has at least one disadvantage!

It is as well, however, to slay the myth that easy answers exist.

Starry-eyed approaches to local action have a poor track-record. They tend to breed disappointment if not disillusionment, to produce big mistakes if not a total disaster and to be less help than expected, if not downright counter-productive. Accepting that there are limits to what you can do is simply common sense.

There are three good reasons why being a realist about local action need not make one a pessimist. The first is that it is often possible for a voluntary group to slot into an umbrella scheme which does most of the paperwork on behalf of the group, and which has plenty of experience in avoiding the major problems. The scheme may be run by the local authority or by a managing agent set up by a group of churches (to give just two examples). Fitting into a wider scheme can save a lot of time and anxiety.

Second, no project is too small. It is better to help one person than nobody. If the group's resources are limited, one can hardly be blamed for working within those limitations! What is open to criticism is the failure to make the most of what the group has, however tiny.

Third, small beginnings can have surprisingly big results. Many of the larger projects in this chapter had a very modest start. In a number of cases their founders never dreamed that they would develop on such a big scale. Time and again people working with the unemployed find that when a group of people without jobs regularly meet together, unexpected reserves of skill and imagination come to the surface. Groups frequently seem to 'take off'. What began as a small drop-in centre grows into a self-help group, a training centre, a provider of temporary and permanent jobs or a combination of these.

So who knows what the result will be when a group of unemployed people meet, learn to trust each other and plan some action? There may be excitement ahead. The important thing is to start.

CHAPTER 8

Personal Action

George is fifty-five years old and lives in the West Midlands. He had worked for a large engineering company for twenty-nine years before being involved in an industrial accident. Now he has only one eye. He knows he 'hasn't a chance' of getting a job 'because employers will always prefer a younger and fitter bloke'. He has been out of work for two years, and says he is frightened of the future. His wife helps a bit, but that is no substitute for the company of workmates. 'You talk to a bloke who's in work now – he's not interested. He doesn't know what it's like. You can't explain to people what it's like. They've got to experience it first... There's no more putting your hand in your pocket and feeling a few coppers and some notes – that's what I can't do anymore. Others don't understand.' George found facing unemployment alone a bitter experience.

Many of the jobless feel the same. Yet they are often surrounded by family, acquaintances in the neighbourhood and friends not far away. It might seem that they have no need to be on their own. Lack of cash of course makes it difficult to take part in social activities, to have a drink in the pub, and this leads to a growing away from friends. But that is not the only reason for isolation. On top of the money miseries is the feeling that others just do not understand.

How well do the employed respond to the unemployed? Do they keep their distance, making the individual feel more worthless and even more rejected? Or do they draw close, ready to share the burden as best they can? Are they ready to give support through acceptance, letting the person talk it out, encouraging them to explore new options, showing them how to discover hope and helping them to take action? For these are five steps to coping with unemployment.

ACCEPTANCE

So how should people approach the jobless? Sometimes those in work have to take the initiative. If a church wanted to work with

159

the unemployed and found that there were very few of them in the congregation, it might have to make a special effort to get in touch with them. Very often, people who have been out of work for a long time retreat into such an isolated existence that it is difficult to reach them at all. Starting a local action group may be the answer. At the other extreme, members of the family may feel that they cannot get away from Dad now that he stays at home all day. And then there are those who have occasional contacts with the unemployed. All may find it difficult to accept the jobless because of embarrassment, misunderstanding or 'inner space invaders'.

Embarrassment

In places where it is normal to have a job, 'What do you do?' is the invariable question on meeting someone for the first time. For the person who does not work and wishes he did, the question can be the psychological equivalent of a punch in the stomach. Not surprisingly, many of the jobless would rather the question was never put. Once it has been asked, though, the situation is frequently made worse by an awkward silence, followed by a faltering attempt to change the subject. This only confirms to the person out of work that it is socially unacceptable to be without a job – so unacceptable, in fact, that no one can talk about it. Another message of rejection comes on top of the countless already received.

If someone decides to make conversation by asking 'What do you do?' they should be prepared to follow though in a way that does not leave the other person feeling uncomfortable. A helpful response on learning that someone is unemployed is to ask an open-ended question on the lines, 'That must be tough. How are you finding it?' This shows the person that you are not trying to avoid the subject, and gives them the opportunity to close off this line of conversation if they wish. On the other hand, if they reply 'pretty awful' in a way that suggests they do not mind talking about it, an appropriate response might be, 'What do you find most difficult?' For those who may not find it easy to respond spontaneously in this way, it can be helpful to imagine oneself in advance holding a conversation along these lines. When one then gets into the situation, one will be less likely to react with embarrassment.

Misunderstanding

Embarrassment may be related to misunderstanding, which is one of the occupational hazards of unemployment. People may have the best will in the world, but their lack of understanding may prevent the jobless from feeling accepted. Their good intentions may betray pity, the last thing the out-of-work need. Or their approach may be paternalistic. They want to do something *for* the unemployed, whereas the jobless want to be treated as partners, not recipients of charity.

Forty-two-year-old Derek, who had a semi-skilled job till the factory closed down, is typical of many in hating the thought of having a drink bought for him without being able to buy one back. 'It's a bit of pride on my side, but if somebody buys me a drink I want to be able to afford to say, "Well have one on me as well'. This is a warning to those with generous hearts that they must show their generosity in sensitive ways. Giving money to the hard-up without providing them with the chance to give something in return should be avoided if at all possible.

Others may be inclined to blame the unemployed. A mother with an out-of-work daugter about the house may say, 'Yes, of course I understand. It's a terrible experience for her.' Yet underneath she is thinking, 'Judith ought to do more to get a job. She's not trying very hard.' Even if it is well disguised, the accusation will not go unnoticed. It will leave the daughter, who is desperate for encouragement, even more dejected. To ask repeatedly, in an attempt to help, whether a person has tried this job or that may only increase their sense of inadequacy. Either they were too demoralized to try, in which case they will feel guilty, or they tried without success, in which case they may feel an utter failure. Still other people may simply not know how to respond to the jobless. 'The problem is not that I am not enjoying it; it is that everyone else thinks I ought not to be enjoying it,' says Jean, a graduate. Attempts to sympathize can reinforce the sadness instead of easing it.

Genuine understanding immediately conveys to the jobless that they are accepted, and knowing that they are valuable enough to be accepted can be a first step to restoring their battered self-esteem. Yet those who have never been unemployed, or quickly found a job when they were out of work, sometimes find it difficult to imagine what prolonged unemployment can be like. Answering questions such as these can be helpful in thinking yourself into the experience of the jobless:

☐ Where is your security? How important are your material possessions, your job?

☐ How would you feel if these were taken away from you, if you woke up tomorrow and found that your job had disappeared?

☐ How would you feel if one person after another said they did not want to employ you; if at one interview you were told that you were over-qualified and at the next that you were not qualified enough; that for most jobs you applied for you were never even told that you had been rejected, and that for the last one you heard that there were over 300 other applicants?

☐ How would you feel if your summer holiday had lasted for fifty-two weeks? Could you still keep yourself busy after all that time, or might you be feeling rather bored?

☐ After rent or mortgage payments, how much do you have to live off each week? If you are a single householder, how would you like to live off £26.80 a week (the 1984 supplmentary benefit rate)? If you are married with two children and an unwaged wife, how would you like to live off £61.80, again the 1984 rate?

☐ How would it feel to be at the receiving end of others' generosity, but never to have the chance to do something worthwhile yourself?

The realization that losing a job can be a form of bereavement is also helpful. Even if you have never been made redundant, you can imagine something of what it is like by recalling your feelings after the loss of someone you loved.

Inner space invaders

Sometimes the failure to accept the unemployed stems from reasons beyond the lack of imaginative understanding. A youth-worker has a particularly busy day ahead of him, yet here is Tom who on past form will talk non-stop for at least an hour. 'How can I get rid of him?' the youth worker asks himself as the minutes tick by. Tom will know that the youth-worker is not listening – another rebuff in a life which is full of them.

Or we may see in the unemployed something that we dislike about ourselves. A young lad's father, just made redundant, appears a failure and his son's fear of failure bubbles up inside. 'Basically aren't I a bit like him?' the young man thinks. 'He reckons he lost his job because his eyesight was going, but really it was because he wasn't good enough... Well, I wonder if I'm good enough...' As the father's vulnerability shakes his son and perhaps vice versa, it is not surprising that they both literally get on each other's nerves.

In another family the sister has lost her job, stirring up unrecognized fears within her brother: 'Her factory had to close. I wonder if redundancy is very far from mine. Perhaps things aren't quite as certain as I thought. I do wish she wouldn't talk like that – it irritates me.' Is it her voice which is irritating, or the reminder that life is not quite as secure as he thought?

Thoughts like these can come between those in work and those out of it. They shift attention away from the other person towards oneself. 'Well, if I'm not important enough to have his attention, I can't be much good,' someone without a job may think. He may angrily respond in ways designed to show the family that he is important, raising the household temperature a few degrees. Or he may walk sadly away from the youth-worker's room, confirmed in his view that if people don't have time to listen, there must be something wrong with him.

Inner space invaders such as the concern about demands on our time, fears that we may be as inadequate as others seem to be, and worry that our job may go next can prevent genuine acceptance of the unemployed. Like so many feelings they have to be faced before they can be faced down, and this can be a painful experience. If we are serious about accepting the unemployed, we must be realistic about the cost this can bring to us personally. We may find ourselves confronted by fears which we had never recognized before.

Coming to terms with anxieties about our ability to cope, our own basic worth and our material security often involves a lengthy struggle similar to that faced by the jobless themselves, as they experience fears of being overwhelmed, loss of self-esteem and loss of security. Wrestling with our own very similar feelings will remind us of our vulnerability. It will help us not only to accept the vulnerability of the other person, but to enter more imaginatively into his or her situation. If a friend's unexpected redundancy threatens my sense of security, then I can imagine more vividly how he must feel now that his security has been shattered.

Sometimes the fears of those alongside the unemployed can be dealt with in quite practical ways. The rushed youth worker may need to explain to Tom his busy programme, assure him that he is not being given the 'brush off' and ask him to come for a chat 'for half an hour' at the same time tomorrow. More often the feelings are too deep-seated to be resolved so easily. Often it helps just to recognize them, or to talk about them with a person you feel safe with. Christians feel they have an added resource – prayer. It is a resource worth mentioning since many churches and Christians do work with the unemployed and do find prayer effective.

In prayer, Christians can learn to wrestle with the fears and insecurities that plague us all. In prayer we can set against our fears of failure, sparked off by someone who has lost her job perhaps, the fact that God accepts us however many times we fail. Or that he loves us enough, despite our failures, to have died for us, and will look after us in the midst of our failure. We can acknowledge that life is insecure, but draw comfort from God's promise to give us strength in our insecurities. We can recognize our limitations, whatever they are, and oppose them with the knowledge that God can help us to overcome them.

Prayer is not something that should be underestimated. It is the natural response of many people in times of trouble, whether they are Christians or appear to have little faith. It is a resource that is available to all who work with the unemployed, as well as to the jobless themselves.

TALKING IT OUT

Acceptance involves a willingness to listen to the jobless. 'People try to care but... You need someone to sit down with you, and help you get out of the confusion. Someone who will listen. One of the first questions people ask is "What do you do?' Usually there's an embarrassed silence, then I say, 'I'm one of the 3 million.' People are fairly sympathetic, but they don't know what it feels like... It's very demoralizing.' The way to find out how this woman feels is to let her talk.

One may then be faced by a kaleidoscope of emotions: despair about ever getting a job, regret at the failure to make the most of previous opportunities, a strong sense that it is unfair, resentment that the best deal society can offer is a raw one, and bitterness at the attitude of family and friends. An older person may express regret that a lifetime of occupational skills has been flushed down the drain, worry that he cannot cope, anger that the reward for years of loyalty was a redundancy note and an acute loneliness. Listening to pent-up feelings and drawing them out can ease the distress, while echoing them back in one's own words will show that the feelings really have been understood. The person will see that they are valuable enough for someone to have taken the trouble to understand.

The listener will need to tune into different emotions according to what stage of the unemployment experience the individual is at. For a workmate getting news of his redundancy, the predominant feelings are likely to be shock, bewilderment and disbelief. A helpful conversation will allow these to be expressed. Well-meaning assurances like 'I'm sure you'll be all right. With your skills you're bound to get a job soon' are likely to discourage a flood of emotion. They may tell the other person that his more fortunate friend cannot handle his shock. Questions such as 'Have you thought about how you are going to cope?' will be even less appropriate. The individual needs to have worked through the shock before turning to more practical thoughts.

But as numbness and the like seem to taper off by the end of the conversation, a question about the next step can be helpful. 'Have you thought how you are going to break the news to your wife?' may start the person thinking about what to do over the next couple of hours. A recent survey found that what the unemployed wanted during the initial stages of being out of work was not so much constructive advice as more general signs of caring and support. The need for advice increases as the experience of unemployment is prolonged.

Frequently, as we saw in chapter one, shock is followed by an optimistic pretence that nothing has changed. Family and friends may be tempted to bring the person down to earth, to encourage them to face the fact that they are not holiday, that the chances of getting a job are pretty bleak and that they had better start looking now before employers say they have been out of work for too long. Relatives may naturally be anxious if redundancy pay is 'blown' on luxuries while outstanding loans remain upaid. 'How will he survive when the money's gone?' they may ask themselves.

On the other hand optimism gives the unemployed person protection against a reality that is still too painful to face. To puncture illusions prematurely can be cruel and unhelpful. Warnings may simply be ignored because the person is not ready to face them. If the individual is going on a spending spree, a more constructive response may be to encourage them subtly (if at all possible) to buy things that will stand them in good stead while out of work. And it will bring relief to draw out their smouldering anger and frustration after the harsh reality of signing-on.

There are cases where optimism is excessively prolonged. An extreme example was a twenty-one-year-old who had been unemployed for four years, but was so convinced that he would get a docker's job (even though there was not a chance) that he refused to look at anything else. Sensitively exploring the feelings which lay behind that certainty – perhaps the fear that he would lose status by not working in the docks – might have helped him to come to terms with reality. For most of the unemployed, though, the search for a job provides an all-too-brutal reminder of the real world. Becoming careless about clothes, appearances or punctuality are often signs that a person's self-esteem is suffering from the emotional wear and tear which results from failure to get a job. Watching out for these and encouraging expressions of hurt after a job-rejection will at least send the message, 'The employer may not care, but I do. You're worth enough for me to care enough to spend time with you.'

The individual may start to accuse him or herself: 'I should have seen it coming. I should have changed jobs while I had the chance.' Bringing these into the open will help the person to recognize their guilt feelings and will eventually make it easier for them to stop condemning themselves. They may not know what they are thinking until they say it. Anger toward those in authority, former workmates, family or the interviewer that morning may come out in destructive ways if it is bottled up. A daughter may be forced to lash out at her mother because there is no other way to express her anger. If the family can possibly create space during the week to listen to it or if there is an attentive ear outside the home, domestic rows might not register quite so highly on the family richter scale.

As the individual enters the phases of despair and resignation, negative feelings will multiply. Clinical depression may set in, which means that she or he ought to see a doctor if they are not doing so already. Friends and relatives should watch out for the tell-tale signs – a prevailing sadness or emptiness, an uncharacteristic tendency to take the worst view of everything, a constant pondering on personal failure, persistant swings of mood from feeling morbid in the morning to feeling better in the evening, a slowing down of behaviour, weight loss (though it may be caused by an inadequate diet), appetite loss and loss of sleep (particularly early waking, though this may be the result of sleep during the day). If several of these signs are present, it may mean that the person is suffering from a depression – a severe case of the 'dole-drums' – which needs medical treatment as well as personal caring.

Ideally, families should be best placed to provide this care. But their own emotional resources may already be stretched to breaking point. Voluntary groups who care for the jobless should try not to forget the families of the unemployed. All too often they are emotionally bruised and battered, too. The wife of an unemployed husband may bear the brunt of his anger, share his fear of the future, experience frustrations over the lack of money, bask in reflected failure and find herself carrying the family as a whole. She may need as much support as her husband. Caring for the family, perhaps by drawing them into a warm and accepting community, may be one of the best ways to help someone out of work. In practice, though, this is more easily said than done.

Everyone's experience of unemployment is different. Listening for what makes the individual's situation unique will underline the extent of your concern. So it is important to show that you understand the frustrations of being a woman in the job market, why the agonies of living at home are so great for the twenty-year-old who should be growing up, why the West Indian feels so discriminated against, how it feels for the fifty-five-year-old to be denied the chance to build up a pension, and so on. For those working specifically among the jobless, it is particularly vital to show that the person is valued for her or himself and not merely as one of the unemployed with a 'typical' problem.

EXPLORING NEW OPTIONS

Listening is not only therapeutic in itself – people feel better after a good talk. It also shows that the listener cares and hopefully understands. Only then will the listener have earned the right to encourage the unemployed person to explore new options, which is the next step in surviving unemployment. The terrain to be covered will include the person's attitudes, their aims and abilities and the alternatives open to them.

Attitudes

How the jobless interpret their situation will greatly influence their ability to make the most of it by exploring new courses of action. Some may feel that it is their fault – that they are failures, worthless and so on. This breeds a resigned attitude along the lines of: 'Well I'm no good, so I can't do anything about it.' Others may deny any responsibility. They may blame the government, trade unions, management, the supervisor who got them the sack, their family or anyone so long as it is not they themselves. This produces an attitude which says, 'I can't do anything about it because it is the fault of everyone else.' One person will feel powerless because he is no good, the second because others are no good. Neither will be likely to respond constructively.

It is asking a lot for people with battered pride to see themselves in a more positive light. Every unacknowledged job application tells them that they are not worth a reply. Government training schemes designed to make them more employable convey the message, however unintentionally, that the unemployed are really to blame. 'There must be something wrong with you,' the schemes say in effect, 'if training is needed to put you right.'

Yet for the great majority, it is not their fault that they have been caught in the roulette wheel of unemployment. If they had been born ten or fifteen years earlier they would almost certainly have had a job. They are unemployed for reasons totally beyond their control: because of the government's failure to speed up economic growth, or because they live in areas where old industries have had to close, or because of deep-seated conflicts within society. Your view will depend on how convinced you are by the different explanations of unemployment. But whatever the view, the jobless are certainly victims of forces which are scarcely understood.

The individual might take comfort from the fact that many others (one in eight people in United Kingdom) are going through a similar experience. Many more have been through it quite recently, and almost everyone will experience a period out of work, albeit short, at some stage in their life. It is not abnormal to be unemployed. Indeed, in some professions, it is an accepted part of life. In 1974, three-quarters of the British actors' union, Equity, were 'resting' on any particular day. Show-biz is a high-status profession. If being forced to rest is good enough for them, need the rest of us feel quite so bad when it happens to us? Remember the cliche (which happens to be true) that it is the job which has been made redundant, not the person.

For the jobless who want to blame everyone else for their situation, it may help to list factors over which they have virtually no control (redundancy, effects of new technologies, level of supplementary benefit, and so on) and things which they fcan control (determination to job-hunt, making the best of the bad situation, and so on). If they feel discouraged because the second list looks much shorter than the first, then some morale-boosting may be necessary: 'Am I going to let it beat me or can I battle through, finding solutions which others thought never existed? Am I going to let my family see me crushed, or can I show them that there is more to me than they thought? They think I'm no good, but I'm overcoming far bigger problems than they have ever faced.'

Thoughts like these may be hard to sustain; they may need encouragement from others in a similar position. But they are important because the unemployed have the chance to show society that suffering need not bring only despair, misery and pain. Just as people admire a handicapped person who struggles triumphantly against the odds, so it will respect the jobless who can overcome the obstacles stacked against them to master their situation.

For all the unemployed, whether they are inclined to blame themselves or other people, it may be useful to list some of the advantages of being out of work. For the first time they may be able to have the chance to do what *they* want to do without being tied down by school, a course, or a job which was not very interesting anyway. (There are probably just as many bored, isolated and depressed people in work as there are out of it!) Their time is no longer organized by someone else – it is under their control. Unemployment is an opportunity to develop a more varied and worthwhile life than a boring job: to do those hobbies you had often planned, to learn that new skill which always seemed so interesting, to spend more time with the family.

The unemployed person may have discovered how a boring job can squeeze out a rich family life, so why not let a rewarding family life squeeze out the need for a boring job? Here is a chance to spend time with the children or grandchildren, to make things together, explore places, play games, tell stories and read books – and it can be done because there is no job to wear you out. J.B. Priestly once remaked, 'I don't think I've ever done a hard day's work in my life, yet I've always done what I've wanted to – which is much cleverer.'

Aims and Abilities

A more positive attitude may come as the unemployed consider their aims. Often the jobless feel thoroughly confused. They are so overwhelmed by what is happening to them that they can hardly think what they would like to do even if they had the chance. A way to get over this would be to write down, perhaps with a friend, what they would *really* like to do but perhaps never thought was possible. This will probably include ideas which feel ridiculous, but actually writing them down will probably reveal something about the person's deepest desires.

Having done this, it may then be worth taking four or five jobs which they would love to do if they had the skills, money or whatever was necessary. They could write down what was attractive about each job, and use the list to spark off thoughts about work and non-work values under the following heads, taken from the very helpful book *How to Survive Unemployment*.

1 **Social** How important is the company of others? Did you miss your workmates a lot after losing your job? How involved in family life are you/do you want to be?
2 **Concern** How important is it to do something useful for society – to be involved in a good cause? Do you enjoy helping others with or without reward?
3 **Money** How keen are you to be free of money worries? Do you want to earn lots of money for yourself or for others?

4 **Success** How keen are you to have responsibility, to use skills and judgement, to accomplish important things?

5 **Power** How important is it for you to be well-known, to lead other people, to influence the thoughts and actions of others?

6 **Learning** How eager are you to seek knowledge or learn new skills?

7 **Variety** How important is it to have a change of activity or scene?

8 **Independence** How vital is it to be your own boss or to do things in your own way, to work alone and at your own pace? Do you like a lot of direction?

9 **Creativity** How keen are you to develop new products or new ideas, or to be doing something artistic?

10 **Lifestyle** What sort of life do you want to lead – to be away from crowds and sophistication or to live near theatres and pubs, to be busy most of the time or to be free of pressures and expectations?

Answering these questions and then listing the ten items in order of importance should enable one to read off priority aims.

Clearly, a person needs the right sort of abilities to achieve his or her aims, but often the jobless underestimate their abilities. They are so dazzled by the importance society attaches to paper qualifications that they forget all about the non-paper skills such as the ability to get on with people. We noted in chapter two that a third of the unemployed men in Britain are labelled 'unskilled' by the experts. The task of proving the experts wrong can start with this exercise from Guy Dauncey's *The Unemployment Handbook*, another useful book.

1 For fifteen minutes, the person makes a brief year-by-year diary of their life so far – what has happened to them, the most important things done, schools attended and so on. This should get the memory going.

2 For the next hour or so the person should list things they have done which have a special sense of satisfaction, made them feel proud or gave them a deep sense of enjoyment. The list might include 'completed five-day hike with friends', 'learnt how to master and handle a new machine', 'worked successfully as foreman for a year', 'won a swimming competition', and so on.

3 The seven achievements which mean most to the person should then be listed – preferably in order of importance.

4 With someone if possible, a list should be made of the skills used in those achievements. They might be considered under four headings – skills related to ideas and information (for example, knowledge, analyzing, compiling and copying), skills related to things or products (for example, handling, making and copying), skills related to people (for example, serving, taking instructions, persuading, advising) and personality traits which do not fit easily into the other categories (for example, persistence). It is important not to overlook the obvious skills. If you drove to work for the year you were a foreman, then 'driving' should be included.

5 The five skills which occur most often or were used in the three top achievements class as the person's chief skills at that moment (it may be possible to add to them). Asking yourself for several weeks, 'What kind of job would enable me to develop or use my skills?' and 'What sort of job would enable me to achieve my aims?' may release a log-jam of ideas.

Friends of an unemployed person should make a special effort to affirm her or his abilities. Often we do not recognize our own qualities till someone else points them out. In any case it is always nice to be told that you are good at something, especially if you are out of work. For the jobless, encouragement is a priceless gift.

Alternatives

The difficult task is to try to match ideas to the few alternatives around. A list of possible jobs can be built up by scanning the papers, talking to friends or visiting the Job Centre (perhaps to show someone the lists of aims and skills and to ask for suggestions). A person might take five possible jobs and imagine themselves doing each one. What would it feel like? What would it feel like after a year? Which aims would the job fulfil and which would it not? Is the idea worth taking further? If so, information from the Job Centre, or phonecalls in response to ads will indicate what skills are required and whether the person has a realistic chance of getting this type of work. Even if the chance is small, the idea should be tucked away. Maybe something can be made of it later.

Going through this process will help people to assess how many of their aims are likely to be realized through a job. They will be extremely fortunate if they can think of a job which will fulfill all their major aims – and even more so if they have a chance of getting it. Many of the unemployed will consider themselves fortunate if there is a remote possibility of a job which satisfies even a few of their aims. They might then advance on two fronts.

They can try to improve their prospects of getting the job (or increase the range of jobs they may be eligible for). They might put in for a training course, get help with job applications and interview techniques, explore moving to another area, or make sure they are first into the telephone box by getting early copies of the local paper as it rolls off the press. People whose motivation is not up to this will need special support from family and friends, who should remember that not everyone has the 'go-getting' streak, and that on the other side of a failure to compete will almost certainly be a quality of some kind – patience perhaps, or sensitivity toward others.

The second front will be to explore ways of fulfilling outside a job aims which are not likely to be satisfied within it. If a person wants to do something creative and the most likely job open to them is a routine one, they might look for other ways of expressing their creativity. Unemployment can be a chance to invest in the future by looking at what is available locally in evening classes, colleges, clubs and societies. The person with no interests should keep looking until something strikes them – computers, dancing, jazz, wood-carving, making clothes or writing poetry. Local courses are often half-price (and occasionally free) to the unemployed. If the course is too expensive, is it possible to help a local craftsperson or cycle repair person, for instance, for two days a week unpaid?

Unemployment can then become a time for developing interests to round out your life when you finally land a job. Boredom without work may be the spur for discovering a more interesting life with work. Also, 'one thing leads to another' – one of the golden rules of unemployment. Working part-time unpaid as a plumber's mate (to learn how to install your own central heating one day) may enable you to become quite skilled. That could eventually lead to a friend-of-a-friend asking you to go into partnership. The car-maintenance course ('just for fun') may be the first step in getting a part-time (and then full-time) job in a garage. Advance on the second front may, unexpectedly, bring victory on the first.

Unfortunately, though, the job famine prevents far too many of the unemployed advancing on the job front at all. There are just no vacancies around. As heroes making the best of an almost impossible situation, they may scour the local paper to see what is going on and get ideas for job-substitutes: summer play-schemes for local children; a drama society looking for designers, carpenters or costume-makers; a badminton or squash club; a local campaign against health-service cuts, and so on. Why not plan a holiday (the unemployed are entitled to them too!) to get a break from home and the hassle of looking for jobs? Workcamps provide hundreds of free opportunities involving residential projects with young teenagers, archaeological digs, and helping the disabled to have a holiday, to name a few. There is no loss of benefit if you do not go abroad. With the imaginative support and encouragement of others, it may in some cases be possible for the unemployed to pioneer a more varied life than if they had a job.

But there will always be the problem of money. The unemployed come back to this time and again. 'The hardest thing for me is that you've got to watch where you're going – the bus fares.' Lack of money for the bus can kill a good idea before it has a chance. (Government really should provide the jobless with cheap fares in off-peak hours). One of the most helpful books on making the most of unemployment is *Nice Work if You Can Get It*, again written by Guy Dauncey. In it Dauncey describes four ways to stretch unemployment pay. The first is called (rather grandly) financial budgeting and control. This includes writing down everything you spend and working out at the end of the week where savings can be made, if necessary. Putting a bit aside into a 'fun budget' can be a way to save for a special treat. The feeling that you can never splash out on anything, or finding that the dole cheque has been frittered away on unplanned luxuries, has a very draining effect.

The second thing is to know your rights. Many people do not draw all the benefit they are entitled to. It is worth checking with others in a self-help group or with the Citizens Advice Bureau. Taking a friend when you have to discuss or argue a point at the social security office will boost your confidence. The third point is to earn up to the limit under benefit rules if at all possible, and to know those rules thoroughly. The rules for unemployment benefit are more generous and flexible than supplementary benefit (there is no limit on Sunday earnings, for example). On top of the £4 supplementary benefit limit, a laughable (but useful) £1 is allowed for expenses.

Dauncey's fourth piece of advice is to live creatively. Brewing one's own beer at a fraction of the pub cost and holding a 'shared feast' (a party to which each person brings some food) can be a cheap and successful way to reduce the cruel isolation of unemployment. Exploring new recipes, looking for the chance to bulk purchase (yet another reason why company is so important for the jobless) and growing your own vegetables can help to slash the food budget. People are often surprised when they hear that a new supermarket has opened in a town with acute unemployment. 'People can't be doing so badly on the dole,' they think. How little they know! What is really happening is that the jobless are switching from the more expensive corner shop to the cheaper, if less convenient, supermarket.

DISCOVERING HOPE

Imagine that George, whom we met at the beginning of the chapter, joins a self-help group where he finds himself accepted and where someone takes the time to listen to his fears and resentments. Talking it out is a turning point – George never realized how much he blamed other people. Recognizing that and asking what areas of his life he did have some control over is the start of a more positive approach to unemployment. He thinks through his aims (quite a revelation – so many unfulfilled after fifty-five years!) and his abilities (more than he thought). He begins to look at the alternatives open to him, but finds that it is hard work to come up with ideas. Often it is harder work trying to survive on the dole than to do a proper job, but George is not the type to worry about that. For him, there is a 'nagging something' that is the real problem. George finds it difficult to put his finger on it, but as he talks it suddenly becomes crystal clear.

'It was easy at first. When I realized that unemployment was an opportunity and that there were some things I could do about it, I began to feel better. As I went through my aims I got quite excited. But then I wrote down my abilities and I began to wonder, 'how many of my aims am I really going to achieve? Now as I look at the alternatives I realize what a con it all was. Money was really high up my list of aims – more than all the power and learning stuff. I need it, not just now, but for my pension. I can't go on for another twenty years with the sort of life I've got. But all these high-sounding alternatives – evening classes, workcamps, visiting the old (that's me!)... where's the money? That's what I want to know. Where's the money coming from?'

A new angle

If this was George's experience, he might look for a new angle on life. The bruised and vulnerable self is always on the look-out for ways of massaging itself. Maybe it wants to ease the pain of insecurity ('what about my pension?'), of feeling incompetent ('there's not much I can do'), or of losing respect ('you're still out of work?'). A job with its pay, the chance to do a task well, and the status it gives, will bring relief. But the relief may be short-lived. After a while the questions may start again. 'Am I really secure? What happens if this place closes like the last?' The questions may go deeper. Am I on top of my job – and if I am, so what? My boy's got all these fancy qualifications, but I never did a degree. I suppose I'm lucky to have a craft job, but engineering crafts aren't what they used to be. People really used to look up to us. But now it's all electronics and stuff. Makes us look pretty ordinary.'

As we found in chapter five, some ideas of the Christian faith may help us here. Many Christians have found that the self is most content when it has forgotten itself and turned its attention to others. As it responds to the needs of the other person its own need to be needed is met. A new kind of status is found – one that comes from being valued because of what you did for another person. Respect comes in a new way. Mother Teresa of Calcutta, who abandoned all status for work among the poor and dying, ended up with one of the highest status symbols of all – a Nobel prize.

Discovering that you are able to help another person can also bring self-confidence. ('Perhaps I'm not so hopeless at things, after all.') As for the thirst for security, preoccupation with others can shift your horizons. 'It's what happens to that person today which counts. I haven't got time to worry about the future. And what does it matter anyway? There are more important things than money.'

Looking for the chance to support others, rather than going over and over the failure to get a job, can help to release the unemployed from the depair which prevents them from making more of the few options open to them. It will express the hope that meaning can be found even in the most intolerable situations.

A new strength

Yet it takes courage to stop pursuing one's self and to make others the priority. George may still be nagged by the question of his pension. Can he really be expected to have the strength to let go of his future? Another person may be filled with self-doubt. Scarred by the isolation of unemployment, they may doubt their ability to do much for another person. Or they may say, 'What will my mates think – going to help in an old people's home and not even being paid. "What's wrong with you then?' they'll ask.' We need strength to abandon the attempt to pacify ourselves.

Zacchaeus is a character from the Bible. We do not know much about him, but he seems to have been a lonely person. He was certainly in an unpopular job. He was a major government official – a chief tax-collector which involved not only getting taxes out of people, but fiddling their assessments so that he could get rich on the side. Everyone could see how rich he had become, which they must have found pretty galling. Though we are not told, it is likely that money (and the job) were being used by Zacchaeus to meet his core needs. The people may not have liked him, but they had to respect him, especially as he was guarded by soldiers. He was good at his job because he had grown very rich. And he had more than enough to save for a rainy day and make himself secure.

Asking him to change his values would have been a tall order. But Jesus, who was something of a local hero, came to town. Out of everyone in the crowd desperate to get a sight of him, it was Zacchaeus whom Jesus spoke to. Zacchaeus was bowled over. It was amazing enough that Jesus actually recognized him (had they ever met?) let alone that he should ask to come to his house. 'Out of all these people, it's my house!' Zaccheus must have thought. Perhaps he felt ten feet tall, which would have been quite something because we are told that he was rather short. From that moment his attitude to possessions changed. He promised to return four times over all the money he had stolen from people and to give half his wealth to the poor. Zacchaeus's values had undergone a revolution. Is it reading too much between the lines to suppose that from then on his needs of acceptance by others, and his sense of competence and security were met more by what he gave to people than by what he took from them? Certainly the story ends with Zacchaeus a happy man. The experience of countless others – both in and out of work – has been the same.

The really good news about unemployment is that it can provoke a Zacchaeus-like revolution in values. The crisis of being without paid work can be the chance to look for new sources of status, respect and security. Indeed, pioneering a more significant life on the dole may have something to teach those with a less enriched life off it. In finding new values for themselves, the out-of-work may be able to offer hope to those in work.

INTO ACTION

After being accepted, talking, exploring and discovering hope comes the fifth step – action. For it is not enough for the jobless to devise a plan of survival. They need to know how to make that plan work. Long spells of nothing produce a life lacking in landmarks. The day becomes unstructured, routine goes to pieces and control over time is lost. To 'get out of your lazy bed' becomes increasingly difficult. The individual may need help in turning ideas into practice. A friend can provide the encouragement to break the task down into concrete steps. 'I'd like to play squash' can become 'I'll go to the library to find out if there's a club, or phone the local authority Youth Office, which should know.'

All the things to be done in the coming week – the shopping, signing-on, buying a paper, visiting a friend, that phone call to the Youth Office and so on – should be made into a plan. The week should be structured so that activities are carried out at particular times. Tasks needed to keep yourself alive (washing and the like) might be scheduled for the mornings, leaving the afternoons for more relaxing activities like reading a book or taking a stroll. Building a work-and-leisure routine into the week will give it a structure more akin to a week at work.

If the number of tasks for the week can be counted on one hand, it may be helpful to find one worthwhile thing to do each day – walking the dog, cleaning the house or whatever. This should be seen as an achievement to be looked forward to (if at all possible),

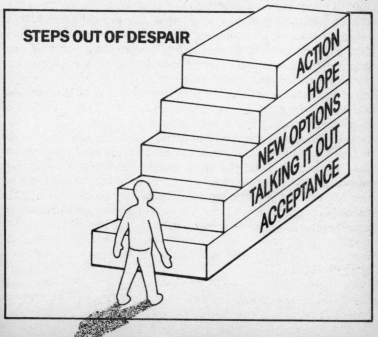

STEPS OUT OF DESPAIR

ACTION
HOPE
NEW OPTIONS
TALKING IT OUT
ACCEPTANCE

and to be planned for a time of the day which particularly drags, perhaps the afternoon which can seem never-ending. It is a good idea to show the plan to a friend who will encourage you to stick to it. Setting long-term objectives for two weeks, six weeks, perhaps three months ahead, can also help. A target date by which you will have learnt to swim, or taught your daughter to drive, will provide some of the challenge that may be found in a job. A structure to the week will help you to be more disciplined and lively, qualities which job interviewers appreciate. And instead of just *thinking* about making the best of unemployment, ideas will have been turned into action.

CONCLUSION

If you are fortunate to work with an unemployed person, it is essential to keep your integrity. The jobless have nothing but contempt for two-faced people in secure jobs who suggest that others should be content with something inferior. There can be no contentment with unemployment. It represents a massive waste and a massive injustice. Survival strategies must never be mistaken for solution strategies. Nor will talk about the unemployed refocusing their lives away from jobs carry much weight from those whose own lives centre on paid work. To agonize with someone with no job, and to do this with integrity, calls for a struggle with your own values. 'Where does my worth lie? Am I hoping this person will do something I'm not prepared to do?' are questions you are bound to ask. Unemployment is a challenge for those in work as well as those out of it.

Yet for those who do walk with the unemployed, the journey can reverse the experience of many jobless. The five stages in the downward spiral of unemployment can be replaced by the five steps to recovery. In place of the shock of losing one's job – the shock of rejection – can come the experience of acceptance. In place of a false optimism which denies reality can come the chance to talk it out. In place of an unsuccessful job hunt, often for work like the old, can come the exploration of new options. In place of despair can be the discovery of hope. And instead of resignation, there can be action. The original experience can be turned into its opposite. Will local and national onslaughts on unemployment make what is possible for one person a reality for many more?

Action Now

For those of us in work, the unemployed are not our problem. We are their problem. Too often we are ignorant, indifferent or unimaginative in the solutions we seek. If we want to stop being the problem, we need to get ourselves informed, commit ourselves to the jobless and be ready for some creative thinking.

Three tasks are absolutely vital. **The first is to care for those without work.** Job-seekers need to be surrounded by a warm and supportive attitude which raises their morale, encourages them to assess their needs for themselves, and helps them to explore how these needs might best be met. It takes time, though, to adjust to painful change. So great sensitivity is required: not to force the jobless to face reality too quickly, but not to encourage them to avoid it either. The unemployed will be helped if they can think creatively about their situation, look at options they had not considered before and structure their days, as far as possible, with worthwhile activities. None of this is easy and it requires great understanding, especially from close friends and relatives. Working with an unemployed person will often involve working with his or her family.

The second task is to catalyze local action. There is much that can and is being done. Voluntary groups in wealthy areas can finance initiatives in high unemployment spots; seminars and conferences can be arranged to raise awareness of local needs; drop-in centres and self-help groups can be started; training schemes set up; temporary and permanent jobs created; or new forms of work or work-sharing can be pioneered. The opportunities are immense – and so too can be the obstacles. A down-to-earth realism, combined with imagination and commitment is vital.

Third, there is the need to communicate. We must counter the confusion and pessimism which exists. It is not true that the best we can do nationally is to go on as we are. The fact is that unemployment can be made to work for us. It provides the chance for government to devise a bold but realistic strategy which will give increasing help to those without a job, and encourage new patterns of work to shape an attractive future.

To those on the right who want more than anything to create a healthy economy, we say: our strategy will do precisely that. It is earthed in economic realities and would have the effect of creating wealth.

To those in the 'soft centre' who say government must increase public spending, we reply: our strategy goes further than that. It show how government spending can be raised in ways that produce most jobs. It is not enough to spend more. Government needs to spend wisely to protect the economy, and imaginatively to generate the maximum number of jobs.

To those on the left who deride the policies of the past and seek a radical approach in tune with the future, we respond: that is at the heart of our strategy. It is designed to build bridges into the new world of work which will confront us in the next century.

To those who want a big vision of the future, we suggest small steps towards it. To those who can see only small steps, we suggest a positive vision to hasten the walk.

Much can be done to combat unemployment. What we need is hope, an exciting vision which keeps both the unemployed and tomorrow in mind, and a willingness by those in work to make sacrifices for those who are not.

Martin Luther King once said, 'We shall have to repent in this generation not so much for the evil deeds of the wicked people, but for the appalling silence of the good people.' What is *our* response to the hope for unemployment – silence?

Resources

FURTHER READING

The following is a selective list of books and articles which were either quoted or proved especially helpful in preparing each chapter.

CHAPTER 1

Coffield F., Borrill C. and Marshall S., 'How Young People Try to Survive Being Unemployed', *New Society*, 64, 2 June 1983

Daniel W.W., *The Unemployed Flow, Stage 1 Interim Report*, Policy Studies Institute 1981

Fagin L., *Unemployment and Health in Families: Case Studies Based on Family Interviews. A Pilot Study*, Department of Health and Social Security 1981

Fagin L. and Little M., *The Forsaken Families*, Penguin 1984

Fryer D., and Warr P., 'Unemployment and Cognitive Difficulties', *British Journal of Clinical Psychology*, 23,1,1984

Gregory P., 'You Don't Heave a Brick Through Your Uncle's Window', *The Guardian*, 18 February 1984

Harrison M., 'How Unemployment Affects People', *New Society*, 67, 19 January 1984

Hayes J., and Nutman P., *Understanding the Unemployed*, Tavistock 1981

Jahoda M., *Employment and Unemployment: a Social-psychological Analysis*, Cambridge University Press 1982

Marsden D., and Duff E., *Workless: Some Unemployed Men and their Families*, Penguin 1975

Piachaud D., *The Dole*, LES Centre for Labour Economics, Discussion Paper No 89 May 1981

Report of Select Committee of the House of Lords on Unemployment, Vols 1 & 2 HMSO 1982

Sinfield A., *What Unemployment Means*, Martin Robertson 1981

Unemployment Unit *Statistical Supplement*, June 1984

Wood S.J. and Cohen J., 'Approaches to the Study of Redundancy', *Industrial Relations Journal* 8,4, 1977-78

CHAPTER 2

Breakwell G.M. and others 'Attitudes Towards the Unemployed: Effects of Threatened Identity' *British Journal of Social Psychology*, 23,1 1984

Brown C., *Black and White Britain: the Third PSI Survey*, Heinemann Policy Studies Institute 1984

Cross M., *Black Unemployment and Urban Conflict*, Aston University 1981

Daniel W.W. *The Unemployed Flow, Stage 1 Interim Report*, Policy Studies Institute 1981

Dex S. *Recurrent Unemployment: Job Separation Reasons and Ethnic Differences in Young Males*, Keele University 1981

'Great Britain Labour Force Estimates for 1983', *Employment Gazette* 92, 8,1984

Jolly J., Creigh S. and Mingay A. *Age as a Factor in Employment*, Department of Employment 1980

Labour Force Survey, 1981

'Labour Market Data' *Employment Gazette* monthly

Lee G. and Wrench J., *In Search of Skill: Ethnic Minorities, Youth and Apprenticeships*, Commission for Racial Equality 1981

Makeham P., *Youth Unemployment: An Examination of Evidence on Youth Unemployment Using National Statistics*, Department of Employment 1980

Martin J. and Roberts C., *Women and Employment: A Lifetime Perspective*, HMSO 1984

Millham S., Bullock R. and Hosie K., 'Juvenile Unemployment: A Concept Due for Re-cycling' *Journal of Adolescence*, 1,1 1978 *1981 Census of Employment*, HMSO 1982

Prais S.J., 'Vocational Qualifications of the Labour Force in Britain and Germany' *National Institute Economic Review*, 98,1981

Prais S.J. and Wagner K., 'Some Practical Aspects of Human Capital Investment: Training Standards in Five Occupations in Britain and Germany' *National Institute Economic Review*, 105 1983

Rankin M., *Strategies for Mutual Support among unemployed people* The Volunteer Centre 1983

'Revised Employment Estimates' *Employment Gazette*, 92,7 1984

Roberts K., Duggan J., Noble M., 'Out-of-school Youth in High Unemployment Areas: an Empirical Investigation' *British Journal of Guidance and Counselling*, 10,1,1982

Sinfield A., *What Unemployment Means*, Martin Robertson 1981

Smith D.J., *Unemployment and Racial Minorities*, Policy Studies Institute 1981

Tiggermann M. and Winefield A.H., 'The Effects of Unemployment on the Mood, Self-esteem, Locus of Control and Depressive Affect of School-leavers' *Journal of Occupational Psychology*, 57,1 1984

Watts A.G., *Education, Unemployment and the Future of Work*, Open University 1983

White M., 'Long-term Unemployment - Labour Market Aspects' *Employment Gazette*, 91,10 1983

CHAPTER 3

The following are written for the non-expert.

Cairncross F. and Keeley P., *The Guardian Guide to the Economy* (in 2 volumes), Methuen 1981,1982

Donaldson P., *Guide to the British Economy*, Penguin 1976

Donaldson P., *Economics of the Real World*, Penguin 1978

CHAPTER 4

Cahill J., 'Swallow Your Pride and Go for that Job' *The Guardian*, 15 August 1984

Elkington J., 'Hanging on for Dear Life' *The Guardian*, 8 March 1984

Freeman C., 'The Kondratiev Long Waves, Technical Change and Unemployment', *Structural Determinants of Employment and Unemployment*, OECD 1979

Gershuny J., *After Industrial Society? The Emerging Self-service Society*, MacMillan 1979

Gershuny J. and Pahl R., 'Work Outside Employment: Some Preliminary Speculations' *New Universities Quarterly*, 34,1 1979/80

Handy C., *The Future of Work*, Blackwell 1984

Interview with Mrs Thatcher *Daily Telegraph*, 5 January 1984

Jenkins C. and Sherman B., *The Collapse of Work*, Eyre Methuen 1979

Jenkins C. and Sherman B., *The Leisure Shock*, Eyre Methuen 1981

Jones B., *Sleepers Wake! Technology and the Future of Work*, Wheatsheaf Books 1982

Manpower Services Commission, *Research Study into the Training Needs and Provisions of User Companies and Office Staff Operating, Managing and Making Use of Text Processing Equipment*, Manpower Services Commission 1982

Northcott J. and Rogers P., *Microelectronics in British Industry: the Pattern of Change*, Policy Studies Institute 1984

Northcott J., Rogers P. and Zechinger A., *Microelectronics in Industry: Manpower and Training*, Policy Studies Institute 1981

Rada J., *The Impact of microelectronics*, International labour Organization 1980

Sinclair, Sir Clive, 'Coming Soon – a Robot Slave for Everyone' *The Guardian*, 24 April 1984

Stonier T., *The Wealth of Information: a Profile of the Post-industrial Society*, Thames Methuen 1983

'Tomorrow's Workers' *The Sunday Times*, 15 April 1984

Watts A.G., *Education, Unemployment and the Future of Work*, Open University 1983

CHAPTER 5

Argrell G., *Work, Toil and Sustenance* Sweden 1976

Bleakey D., *Work: the Shadow and the Substance* SCM 1983

Dow G., 'What Place Does Work Have in God's Purpose?' *Anvil* 1,2 1984

Geldard M., *Encyclopedia of Christian Ethics*, Nelson 1985

Geldard M., '2001 – A Factory Odyssey: Work, Theology and Industrial Revolution' *Anvil*, 2,1 1985

Khaleedee O. and Miller E., 'Jobs: the Great Debate' *The Guardian*, 11 April 1984

Kumar K., 'The social Cultures of Work: Work, Employment and Unemployment as Ways of Life' *The New Universities Quarterly*, 34,1 1979/80

Marshall P. (editor), *Labour of Love: Essays on Work*, Toronto 1980

Moltmann J., 'The First Liberated Man in Creation' *Theology and Joy* SCM 1973

Richardson A., *The Biblical Doctrine of Work*, SCM 1963

CHAPTER 6

Coping With Unemployment, Economist Intelligence Unit 1982

Dilnot A.W., Kay A.J., Morris C.N., *The Reform of Social Security*, Institute of Fiscal Studies 1984

Luton M., 'The Insiders' Guide to a Labour Nightmare', *The Guardian*, 24 February 1984

Morrell J., *Employment in Tourism*, British Tourist Authority 1982

Of Benefit to All, National Consumer Council 1984
Policies for Recovery, Cambridge Econometrics Ltd 1981
Report of Select Committee of the House of Lords on Unemployment volumes 1 & 2 HMSO 1982
Sheppard D., 'The 1984 Richard Dimbleby Lecture', *The Listener* 19 April 1984
Stonier T., *The Wealth of Information: a Profile of the Post-industrial Economy*, Thames Methuen, 1983
Unemployment: a Challenge for us All, Confederation of British Industry 1982

CHAPTER 7

Action on Unemployment (1984) Church Action with the unemployed, 146 Queen Victoria Street, London EC4V 4BX
Beating Unemployment: a Practitioner's Handbook (1984) Centre for Employment Initiatives, 140a Gloucester Mansions, Cambridge Circus, London WC2H 8PA
Connor J., *Bristol Women's Workshop* (1982) Employment Unit, NCVO, 26 Bedford Square, London WC1B 3HU
Dale P., 'Projects Founded by Government: Advice for Christian Organizations in Urban Areas' (1983) The Shaftesbury Project, 8 Oxford Street, Nottingham NG1 5BH
Dauncey G., *Nice Work if You Can Get It* (1982) National Extension College, 18 Brooklands Ave, Cambridge CB2 2HN
Dauncey G., *The Unemployment Handbook* (1983) National Extension College
Green W., *The Christian and Unemployment*, Mowbray 1982
Hannah D., *Work and Unemployment* (1981) The Mission of St James and St John, 8-12 Batman Street, West Melbourne, 3003, Australia
Hunter B. and Manley P., *A Guide to Voluntary Work: Long-term Places* (1983) National Youth Bureau, 17-23 Albion Street, Leicester LE1 6GD
101 Ideas for the Community Programme (1982) Community Task Force, Lowthian House, Preston PR1 2EJ
Rankin M., *Strategies for Mutual Support Among Unemployed People* (1983) The Volunteer Centre, 29 Lower King's Road, Berkhamsted, Herts HP4 2AB
Toynbee P., 'Instant Muscle, Instant Employment' *The Guardian*, 7 February 1983 (for further details write to: Instant Muscle, c/o Rank Xerox (UK) Ltd, Cambridge House, Oxford Road, Uxbridge UB8 1HS)

Two Nations: One Gospel? (1981) Home Mission, Methodist Church, 1 Central Buildings, London SW1H 9NH

Unemployment: Apathy or Action? (1982) The Sydney Christian Youth Network, Anglican Youth Department, 1st Floor, St Andrew's House, Sydney Square, Australia NSW 2000

'Voluntary and Community Organisations and Long-term Unemployment' (1983) National Council for Voluntary Organizations, 26 Bedford Square, London WC1B 3HU

CHAPTER 8

Charley J., *Pastoral Support for the Unemployed*, Grove Pastoral series no 19 1984

Dauncey G., *Nice Work if You Can Get It*, National Extension College 1983

Dauncey G., *The Unemployment Handbook*, National Extension College 1983

Francis L.J., *Young and Unemployed*, Costello 1984

Green W., *The Christian and Unemployment*, Mowbray 1982

Kirby J., *Work After Work*, REACH 1984

Nathan R. and Syrett M., *How to Survive Unemployment*, Institute of Personnel Management 1981

LOCAL ACTION: WHERE TO GET HELP

British Unemployment Resources Network, 318 Summer Lane, Birmingham B19 6RL

Centre for Employment Initiatives, 140A Gloucester Mansions, Cambridge Circus, London WC2H 8PA

Citizens Advice Bureaux

Church Action With the Unemployed, 146 Queen Victoria Street, London EC4V 4BY

Community Relations Councils which are especially glad to help black groups

Local authorities get in touch at an early stage with the person, or team, who acts as a focus of contact with voluntary groups – often part of Chief Executive department. Apart from giving information about funding and so on, he could alert you to planning and other problems.

Local Councils for Voluntary Service will have information on national schemes of funding and non-government sources of finance. Will also know about other groups in the field, and local opportunities generally.

Local enterprise agencies (under various names) mainly interested in helping small businesses, and have useful contacts in local business.

Local offices of **Manpower Services Commission** and **Department of the Environment** for more detailed advice of government funds.

Voluntary Services Unit at the Home Office and the **Inner Cities Unit** of the National Council of Voluntary Organizations. May guide you to the right person if you want to make contact with a government department or another national organization.

This list is not exhaustive. Having started, you quickly learn about others who can help.

Manpower Services Commission:
    Community Industry
    Community Programme
    Voluntary Project Programme
    Youth Training Scheme

Department of Health and Social Security:
    Opportunities for Volunteering

Department of the Environment:
    Special Grants Programme
    The Urban Programme

Rural Community Council, Council for Small Industries in Rural Areas:
    (give grants for rural initiatives)

The Prince's Trusts

Local Authorities

Local Companies

Beating Unemployment, published by the Centre for Employment Initiatives, has a particularly useful section on where to get help.